Perspectives
on
Prayer

by

David Hocking

Promise Publishing Co. Orange CA 92667

Perspectives on Prayer
Copyright 1991 by Promise Publishing Co.
Orange CA 92667

Edited by M. B. Steele

Printed in the United States of America

Scripture is from The Holy Bible, New King James Version,
Copyright 1984 by Thomas Nelson, Inc., Publisher.

Library of Congress Cataloging-in-Publication Data

Hocking, David
        Perspectives on Prayer

ISBN 0-939497-25-5

The

prayer

of

the upright

is

His delight.

Proverbs 15:8

Table of Contents

Foreword

Foreword

Prayer is essential for the spiritual development of our Christian lives. It's easy to think that we can live without it. We learn to trust ourselves rather than God.

Prayer should come before any other ministry. It is first!

By prayer we indicate our dependency on God. Don't try to live your life without a daily appointment with Him!

My prayer is that this book will be a source of encouragement to you in learning how to pray.

David Hocking

Chapter One

WHAT IS PRAYER?

Therefore I exhort first of all that supplications, prayers, intercessions, and giving of thanks be made for all men, for kings and all who are in authority, that we may lead a quiet and peaceable life in all godliness and reverence. For this is good and acceptable in the sight of God our Savior, who desires all men to be saved and to come to the knowledge of the truth. For there is one God and one Mediator between God and men, the Man Christ Jesus, who gave Himself a ransom for all, to be testified in due time, for which I was appointed a preacher and an apostle—I am speaking the truth in Christ and not lying—a teacher of the Gentiles in faith and truth. Therefore I desire that the men pray everywhere lifting up holy hands, without wrath and doubting (I Tim. 2:1-8).

There was a preacher in the fourth century A.D. who was called, "Golden Mouth". His name was Chrysostom and he was one of the most eloquent preachers of all time. In fact, the translation of his writings into English is indeed beautiful to read. He was a man with an enormous vocabulary and he had a way of painting pictures that would draw us to the heart of God. His name is one of the leading names in all of church history. He had a tremendous impact on the people of his own time. I'm quoting something he said in the fourth century about prayer,

> "The potency of prayer hath subdued the strength of fire. It hath bridled the rage of lions, hushed anarchy to rest, extinguished wars, appeased the elements, expelled demons, burst the chains of death, expanded the gates of heaven, assuaged diseases, repelled frauds, rescued cities from destruction, stayed the sun in its course, arrested the progress of the thunderbolt. Prayer is an all-sufficient panoply, a treasure undiminished, a mine which is never exhausted, a sky unobscured by clouds, a heaven unruffled by storm. It is the root, the fountain, the mother of a thousand blessings."

It's beautifully stated, but some of us may still be saying, "What did he say?" What he said is, "Prayer is fantastic!"

PRAYER IS THE PRIVILEGE AND THE RESPONSIBILITY OF EVERY BELIEVER IN JESUS CHRIST

When you first become a Christian, you have this awesome feeling that somebody, at some meeting is going to call on you to pray. If you're not skilled in it, you may feel intimidated especially if you've been around those who begin a prayer with, "Oh, Great Architect of the Universe ..." Some people are scared to death to pray. They don't know how to start.

I remember the joy of leading a man to Christ many years ago who was an attorney. Words were his stock in trade, especially legal terminology. He is now on the Supreme Court of the State of Ohio. I remember when I tried to teach him how to pray. I asked him to get on his knees. "Do we have to?" he asked. He's a large man like I am, and I pushed him down and told him that we need to learn that we are humble before God. Next, he asked how to start and I suggested that he say, "Lord." He said it while looking me straight in the eye. I told him we usually close our eyes when we pray. When he wanted to know why again, I explained that it helps us to keep from thinking of other things. He wanted to know why we should bow our heads, too. It was funny to talk to him about prayer because I had to guide him in every detail through that first prayer. I suggested he just pray what was on his heart, but I'll never do that again! He had to learn how to pray. Later, I called on him to pray in a public meeting and I shouldn't have done that because he wasn't really ready for it. He was in the habit of swearing and he used it in his prayer! When he finished, and I crawled out from under my chair, I said, "Isn't the grace of God wonderful?" I was totally embarrassed in front of the church!!

It's not easy to pray. If anyone tells you that, they probably don't pray much. It may be easy to say some words you've heard other people say, but it's not easy to pray. Every Christian should understand, however, that whether you're a brand new child of God or you've known the Lord for many years, prayer is the privilege and responsibility of EVERY believer. There is something that I don't understand (unless it comes from the enemy) that tells us that prayer is a heavy trip. It's a big hassle—a difficult discipline. There are aspects of it that make it difficult but we need to start with the fact that it is a wonderful privilege and a responsibility of every single believer.

We Have Direct Access to God Through the Work of Jesus Christ

We can never hear often enough that we have direct access to God through the work of Jesus Christ and we can go to God ourselves. We don't have to go through anyone else.

> ... *that He might reconcile them both* [Jew and Gentile] *to God in one body through the cross ... For through Him we both have access by one Spirit to the Father* (Eph. 2:16,18).

So we see that it is through the cross of Jesus Christ that we now have access, by one Spirit, to the Father.

> *Therefore, brethren, having boldness to enter the Holiest by the blood of Jesus, by a new and living way which He consecrated for us, through the veil, that is, His flesh, and having a High Priest over the house of God, let us draw near with a true heart in full assurance of faith, having our hearts sprinkled from an evil conscience and our bodies washed with pure water* (Heb. 10:19-22).

Since He has cleansed us, we have access, so let us draw near. This is an invitation to all of us, *"Draw near"*. I love it when God speaks about access and He uses the words, *"Draw near"*. He could have said, "Come any time you want." He could have said, "You can come, but stand by the door." He could have said, "Remember, there is a great gulf between you and Me, so don't get too close." But God never said any of that! He said, "Draw near". The Bible says, *"Draw near to God and He will draw near to you."*

What a neat thing to understand that prayer not only gives us access to God, but also gives us the ability to sense the closeness of God. A lot of us feel like God is a long way away—He's not personal and real to us even though we believe in Him. Wouldn't you like to have a warm, personal relationship with God? Wouldn't you like to have Him for your best Friend? He will be with you all the time. You can continually talk with Him all the time and wherever you are. *"Draw near to God and He will draw near to you."* That's a wonderful promise we find in James 4:8.

We Are Invited by the Lord to Pray

This blesses me even though it is a simple point. We are literally invited by our Lord Jesus Christ to pray to Him, to talk to Him. You say you love Him, well then talk to Him! Many people don't seem to know what to say to Him, but He wants you to talk to Him—He wants you to pray! Jesus said,

> *"And I say to you, ask* [keep on asking], *and it will be given you; seek* [keep on seeking], *and you will find; knock* [keep on knocking], *and it will be opened to you. For everyone who asks receives, and he who seeks finds, and to him who knocks it will be opened. If a son asks for bread from any father among you, will he give him a stone? Or if he asks for a fish, will he give him a serpent instead of a*

fish? Or if he asks for an egg, will he offer him a scorpion? If you then, being evil, know how to give good gifts to your children, how much more will your heavenly Father give the Holy Spirit to those who ask Him!" (Lk. 11:9-13).

Jesus said, "Ask! It will be given to you!" How simple can He put it? We get ourselves into big trouble all the time and we forget that God has invited us to pray—to call upon Him!

*Let us therefore come boldly to the throne of grace, that we may obtain **mercy*** [God holding back the judgment we deserve] *and find **grace*** [God giving us the forgiveness we do NOT deserve] *to help in time of need* (Heb. 4:16).

If I read that correctly, whenever I have a need, the Bible invites me to talk to the Lord about it. That's exciting, isn't it? I like to put it this way: God never gets tired of my saying "Help!" Some people have felt that because they have asked for other things, and God has so many people to answer, they shouldn't ask for anything more—at least for a while. Just a minute! He's the Eternal God! His understanding is infinite! He says, "Talk to Me! Ask me!"

I heard an oldtime evangelist speak on prayer. He wrote a wonderful book on prayer before he died. He said that prayer is asking and receiving. He emphasized that most Christians do not have what they need because they don't ask! That's what James says, *"You have not because you ask not."* Then, when we do ask, we sometimes ask for selfish reasons instead of for the glory of God. God isn't trying to keep things from you—God wants to give you good gifts.

Jesus told us that in Luke 11. God wants to bless us more than we want to be blessed. God wants to use you more than you want to be used. God says, "Ask Me, and watch! You'll see what I will do." A lot of us are hurting because we've never asked.

Are you troubled? Ask Him for peace. Are you lacking in love for somebody? Ask Him to fill your heart with love for that person. Are you having trouble with bitterness? Ask Him to take it away. Are you having trouble with depression? Ask Him to give you joy. Jesus said,

> *"Hitherto you have asked NOTHING in my Name, ask and you shall receive that your joy may be full"* (Jn. 16:24).

The Lord INVITES us to pray. Ask Him, and it will be given to you, the Bible says. He's not going to give you something you don't want or need. God is always going to give you EXACTLY what you need! Sometimes we don't like what He gives us only to find out later, that was exactly what we needed. The Lord is so good! He knows exactly what He's doing.

We Are Commanded to Pray At All Times

This is another simple point but something that we continue to ignore. Think about it! Do you pray continually about all matters in your life? Prayer is not just a wonderful privilege; it is a great responsibility. God invites us to come, and when you think about it, it is amazing that we don't come. God tells us what He will do.

Then He spoke a parable to them, that men al-
ways ought to pray and not lose heart (Lk. 18:1).

The number one reason we stop praying is because we
get discouraged.   There are several reasons we get discouraged.

We get discouraged when God doesn't answer our
prayers the way we want Him to. When we don't get what
we pray for right away, we give up saying, "What good is
prayer?" Jesus said we should ALWAYS pray and not lose
heart.

We often get discouraged because **circumstances
around us are contrary** to what we've been praying. We
ask for patience and all hell breaks out! If you read the
Bible correctly, you'll see that God is answering your prayer
whether you know it or not. A lot of us don't seem to understand how God works and He answers our prayers the
way He sees fit, not the way we want it. We have a tendency to get discouraged.

We also are discouraged from praying because **it seems
too easy!** What a strange thing. Some people have told me
they have a terrible problem and I offered to have a word of
prayer with them. Some of them actually have gotten mad
at me when I do that. "What are you going to do? If you
say a little prayer, do you think everything will go away?"
It's as though I should have some wonderful counsel to
solve their problem. Wait a minute! Are they trying to say
that it is more important to talk to someone else than it is to
talk to the Lord about your problem?

An insight about counselling I'd like to share with you is that there is a biblical gift of counsel. We all need counsel, but one thing we've done in our generation is to substitute counselling for prayer. I see it everywhere! People don't want to pray, they want someone to give them the answer to their problems as though all that matters is what the counselor thinks! No, we need to PRAY. God answers PRAYER.

A few years ago in Arizona, they had a massive meeting of the American Psychology Association with psychologists and psychiatrists—over five thousand of them. They had done an extensive research project over a number of years with two study groups. One group had gone for counselling, the other hadn't although they had similar problems. The result of the study was published in the newspaper. It said that your chances of getting better are greater if you don't go for counselling! I didn't say that—they did! Thank God, there are some biblical counsellors out there, but we are missing the boat by not praying. If you'd get on your knees and pray about your children and your marriage and your finances and other problems, things would change.

Bob Moorehead, a pastor friend of mine at Overlook Christian Church in Seattle, said he had an old man in his church who really loved to pray. He was a strange man, but he loved to pray. He drove a Gremlin which was a wierd little car, and it was always breaking down. One rainy day, the old man was driving Bob to a meeting and they were on a freeway when the car stopped in the fast lane. Trucks were whizzing by and Bob was alarmed about the traffic and worried about being late for the meeting but the old man said, "This happens all the time." He got out and called Bob to come join him near the hood of the car. He put his hands on the hood and Bob thought the guy was throwing up! He told Bob to put his hands on the car, too, and he wanted to pray for the car to be healed! Bob said he really felt stupid while the old man prayed and he was thinking about how to straighten him out on the subject of prayer when they got back into the car. The man said, "God, you know everything about a Gremlin. You know what's wrong with it and you can heal it. We thank you for this victory." They got back in the car and the car started immediately!

The next day, Bob took his car in for the smog emission test and it didn't pass so he went home, drove into the garage and shut the door so no one could see. He walked up to the car and put his hands on it, then he decided to be specific and put his hand on the tailpipe. The funniest thing is that, when he took it back to the mechanic, it passed the smog test! Bob concluded that he would never doubt that God answers prayer again. It seems to me that God has a sense of humor!

Praying always with all prayer and supplication in the Spirit (Eph. 6:18).

Pray without ceasing, in everything give thanks; for this is the will of God in Christ Jesus for you (I Thess. 5:17-18).

"Men ought always to pray and not to lose heart." Do you get the point?

It's amazing how sophisticated you can get when you know a lot about the Bible. You have all the answers. You begin to think it is childish and naive to pray about the little things in life. God help us! Prayer is the wonderful privilege and the responsibility of every believer. We have direct access to God. We're invited to pray and we're commanded to pray AT ALL TIMES and in every situation. It is NOT meaningless acitivity.

PRAYER IS THE COMMUNICATION OF THE BELIEVER WITH GOD

There are nine different Greek words in the New Testament for prayer and we could really get into the depths of this, but I'm trying to make it as simple as possible. Prayer is communication and it includes at least four things.

Prayer Is Praise

The first thing I want to talk about is praise. You ask me what prayer is and I answer, "Prayer is praise."

When you start to pray, no matter what the occasion is, start with praise! The Lord inhabits the praise of His people. The Lord is delighted with His people who praise Him. It is beautiful to praise the Lord. It pleases Him. Speak of the character of God and how wonderful He is; bless Him with all of your heart.

"Bless the Lord, all that is within me, bless His holy name" (Ps. 103:1).

I will bless the Lord at all times; His praise shall continually be in my mouth. My soul shall make its boast in the Lord; The humble shall hear of it and be glad. Oh, magnify the Lord with me, And let us exalt His name together (Ps. 34:1-3).

Praise the Lord! Praise, O servants of the Lord, Praise the name of the Lord! Blessed be the name of the Lord from this time forth and forevermore! From the rising of the sun to its going down The Lord's name is to be praised (Ps. 113:1- 3).

Some people get upset when they run into a Christian who is singing praises all the time. "Isn't the weather great? Praise the Lord!" What's for lunch? What time is it? Where are you going to eat? All these questions are answered beginning with "Praise the Lord!" Have you met anybody like that? Maybe you think that is just a put-on. I think that since we aren't praising the Lord like we should, it might be a good thing to begin every sentence with "Praise the Lord!" How can we be judgmental about someone who keeps saying this all the time? If I read this right, we all should be doing it!

From the rising of the sun to its going down The Lord's name is to be praised (Ps. 113:3).

Do you praise the Lord all the time? That is prayer!

You are my God, and I will praise You; You are my God, I will exalt You (Ps. 118:28).

I will praise You with my whole heart; Before the gods I will sing praises to You. I will worship toward Your holy temple, And praise Your name For Your lovingkindness and Your truth; For You have magnified Your word above all Your name.

>*In the day when I cried out, You answered me,
>And made me bold with strength in my soul* (Ps.
>138:1).

That's prayer, but it is filled with PRAISE!

>*I will extol You, my God, O King; And I will
>bless Your name forever and ever. Every day I will
>bless You, And I will praise Your name forever and
>ever. Great is the Lord, and greatly to be praised;
>And His greatness is unsearchable* (Ps. 145:1-3).

Prayer is the communication of the believer with God
and it keeps him praising God for everything, for all that is
taking place, and for all the wonderful character of God.

>*Let them praise the name of the Lord, For His
>name alone is exalted; His glory is above the earth
>and heaven* (Ps. 148:13).

>*Praise the Lord! Praise God in His sanctuary;
>Praise Him in His mighty firmament! Praise Him
>for His mighty acts; Praise Him according to His ex-
>cellent greatness! Praise Him with the sound of the
>trumpet; Praise Him with the lute and harp! Praise
>Him with the timbrel and dance; Praise Him with
>stringed instruments and flutes! Praise Him with
>loud cymbals! Praise Him with clashing cymbals!
>Let everything that has breath praise the Lord.
>Praise the Lord*! (Ps. 150:1-6).

You're not PRAYING, if there is no PRAISE!

We're so quick to begin bringing our requests to the Lord
(and God invites us to do that), but PRAYER IS PRAISE!
Praise the name of the Lord!

Prayer Is Thanksgiving

Prayer is also thanksgiving. Sometimes praise and thanksgiving are blended together, but there is a difference. You can praise the character of God without being thankful for what He is doing in your life. There's a great hindrance to prayer when we are not thankful. If there is something in our life that has left us with a root of bitterness or disappointment, and the flow of thanksgiving has dried up, prayer is hindered.

I will offer to You the sacrifice of thanksgiving, And will call upon the name of the Lord (Ps. 116:17).

In our materialistic culture, we don't know about thanking God for the things we don't have. Our thanksgiving seems always to be based on "more". When are we going to thank God for what we **don't** have? In our greedy society, we always want more of everything. Then, **maybe** we'll thank the Lord when it is "enough", but I don't think so.

Be anxious for nothing, but in everything by prayer and supplication, with thanksgiving, let your requests be made known to God; and the peace of God, which surpasses all understanding, will guard your hearts and minds through Christ Jesus (Phil. 4:6-7).

That's simple to figure out. Why aren't we at peace? Because we don't pray? Yes, but also because we don't pray WITH THANKSGIVING when we do pray.

We read from I Thessalonians 5, *"Pray without ceasing"*. It goes on to say, *"In everything give thanks; for this is the will of God in Christ Jesus for you." " ... **everything** ... "* that happens is an occasion to give thanks.

I've had some weeks in which God has done some marvelous things. However, whenever God blesses, the devil works overtime to defeat our spirits. Sometimes, it's unbelievable! One week, a policeman had the audacity to give me a ticket for speeding! Can you imagine that? Then, I got into my car after an out-of-town meeting and, thinking that everyone was gone, I put it into reverse and drove right into a guy's van. That didn't bless me. "In everything give thanks." We went to have a meal with an elderly couple and their window didn't work. He asked me to open the window and I kind of hit it so that it would move, and my hand went through it and I had stitches all along the side of my hand. I was in pain and we couldn't stop the bleeding. I had to spend that night in the hospital! Even that was a Catholic hospital and I'm a Protestant! The doctor came in and said, "Hi! I'm the Pope—Dr. Pope!" No kidding! I was about to leave if he told me his name was John Paul! Next a football coach type came into the room to stitch my hand up. He didn't have on doctor's garb and I couldn't believe my eyes. We were kidding around and I said he must have had "Teasing 101" while he was in college. "No," he said, "Malpractice 303." I didn't seem too funny at the time. When I asked his name, he said, "Dr. Slasher"! That wasn't a good week. At the airport, coming home, I hit another van that I thought was parked but moved instead, and a cop was watching! It's not easy to give thanks in everything during that kind of week. That's when we need to do it most.

A lot of us are playing games. Are you praising the Lord from *"the rising of the sun to its going down"*? Are you really thanking God for everything that happens to you? My natural tendency is built the other way! And so is yours.

Therefore by Him let us continually offer the sacrifice of praise to God, that is, the fruit of our lips, giving thanks to His name (Heb. 13:15).

You may say that it sounds foolish to you. Suppose your car breaks down and you're trying to find the divine reason for that circumstance. If someone comes by and you can witness to them, it's easy. But if nobody comes by, or the money to pay for the repairs doesn't come in and you have to pay the bill, it gets harder to praise the Lord. The worse things get, the harder thanksgiving is. You should have started with thanksgiving! You should have begun when the car broke down, even if you didn't like it and even if you never find out the reason God sent that trial into your life.

Prayer is Confession

At the evening sacrifice I arose from my fasting; and having torn my garment and my robe, I fell on my knees and spread out my hands to the Lord my God, and said, "O my God: I am too ashamed and humiliated to lift up my face to You, my God; for our iniquities have risen higher than our heads, and our guilt has grown up to the heavens. Since the days of our fathers to this day we have been very guilty, and for our iniquities we, our kings, and our priests have been delivered into the hand of the kings of the lands, to the sword, to captivity, to plunder, and to humiliation, as it is this day. And now for a little while grace has been shown from the Lord our God, to leave us a remnant to escape, and to give us a peg in His holy place, that our God may enlighten our eyes and give us a measure of revival in our bondage. For we were slaves. Yet our God did not forsake us in our bondage; but He extended mercy to us in the sight of the kings of Persia, to revive us, to repair the house of our God, to rebuild its ruins, and to give us a wall in Judah and Jerusalem. And now, O our God, what shall we say after this? For we have forsaken Your commandments (Ezra 9:5-10).

Here was a man who was confessing his sin and the sins of his nation along with the sins of his forefathers. Ezra confessed sin and so did Nehemiah.

Please let Your ear be attentive and Your eyes open, that You may hear the prayer of Your servant which I pray before You now, day and night, for the children of Israel Your servants, and confess the sins of the children of Israel which we have sinned against You. Both my father's house and I have sinned. We have acted very corruptly against You, and have not kept the commandments, the statutes, nor the ordinances which You commanded Your servant Moses. Remember, I pray, the word that You commanded Your servant Moses, saying, "If you are unfaithful, I will scatter you among the nations, but if you return to Me, and keep My commandments and do them, though some of you were cast out to the farthest part of the heavens, yet I will gather them from there, and bring them to the place which I have chosen as a dwelling for My name." O Lord, I pray, please let Your ear be attentive to the prayer of Your servant, and to the prayer of Your servants who desire to fear Your name (Neh. 1:6-9,11).

Unless we know about that kind of praying we can't experiencing the blessing of God. Proverbs 28:13 says that if we **confess** and **forsake** our sin, we'll find compassion from the Lord, but if we try to cover up our sin, we will not prosper. The blessing and power of God in your life are quenched at the moment you refuse to confess your sin.

I acknowledged my sin to You, And my iniquity I have not hidden. I said, "I will confess my transgressions to the Lord," and You forgave the iniquity of my sin. For this cause everyone who is godly shall pray to You In a time when You may be found; surely in a flood of great waters They shall not come near him. You are my hiding place; You shall preserve me from trouble; You shall surround me with songs of deliverance (Ps. 32:5-7).

For I acknowledge my transgression, And my sin is ever before me. Against You, You only, have I sinned, And done this evil in Your sight—That You may be found just when You speak, And blameless when You judge. Behold, I was brought forth in iniquity, And in sin my mother conceived me. Behold, You desire truth in the inward parts, And in the hidden part You will make me to know wisdom (Ps. 52:3-6).

The sacrifices of God are a broken spirit, A broken and a contrite heart—These, O God, You will not despise (Ps. 52:17).

Anyone who comes with pride to the Lord, as though he were doing the Lord a favor by praying, had better get right with the Lord immediately. God is very strong in His Word about confession.

Search me, O God, and know my heart; Try me, and know my anxieties; And see if there is any wicked way in me, And lead me in the way everlasting (Ps. 139:23-24).

Are you open to that like David was? Is that what you desire? Are you willing to have God expose the secrets of your life? After all, *"all things are naked and open in the eyes of Him with whom we have to do"*, so you have no secrets from Him! God wants YOU to admit it and pour it out before Him—to confess your transgressions, to confess your sins to Him. He doesn't need this! YOU have the **need to confess** before Him. Some of us never see God bless because there has been no real confession before God.

Prayer is Petition

We give our requests to God—that, too, is prayer.

The righteous cry out, and the Lord hears, And delivers them out of all their troubles. The Lord is near to those who have a broken heart, And saves such as have a contrite spirit. Many are the afflictions of the righteous, But the Lord delivers him out of them all (Ps. 34:17-19).

Isn't it wonderful, what God can do in prayer? Call upon the Lord! He hears and He WILL deliver you. That's what the Bible says!

I love the Lord, because He has heard My voice and my supplications. Because He has inclined His ear to me, therefore I will call upon Him as long as I live (Ps. 116:1- 2).

Do you talk to the Lord like that? Is **that** your relationship to God? *"He has heard ... He has inclined His ear; therefore, I will call upon Him as long as I live."* Do you say, "I'll never stop coming to Him with my petitions and my requests"?

I cry out to the Lord with my voice; With my voice to the Lord I make my supplication. I pour out my complaint before Him; I declare before Him my trouble (Ps. 142:1-2).

Hear my prayer, O Lord, give ear to my supplications! In Your faithfulness answer me, And in Your righteousness (Ps. 143:1).

God wants you to bring your requests to Him!

Be anxious for nothing, but in everything by prayer and supplication, with thanksgiving, let your requests be made known to God (Phil. 4:6).

Now this is the confidence that we have in Him, that if we ask anything according to His will, He hears us. And if we know that He hears us, whatever we ask, we know that we have the petitions that we have asked of Him (I Jn. 5:14-15).

A young man on my staff had been renting a house and he and his wife were asked to leave it because the people that owned it were coming back unexpectedly. The young couple had expected to be in it longer than they were. They were very concerned because their rent money was a limited amount and it was very difficult to find rentals in their area. This young man had the wisdom to pray and he said, "God doesn't do anything crummy!" There was no way he could get another house in his area for the amount of money he had been paying. God put it on someone's heart to rent him a house for the amount of money he had. It was beyond their dreams for a home, but even more than that, this young couple was excited to see how God answered prayer for them. He answered in a miraculous way. They were about to start looking for a house when the phone rang and a man offered to rent them his house. God answered their prayer! It was a really nice house! God wants to bless the socks off of you! God wants to bless you more than you want to receive His blessings.

God doesn't wait in heaven with a baseball bat to club us for every false move we make. As high as our iniquities are, His mercy is much higher. God wants to bless us. He wants to **forgive us** and **deliver us** out of our troubles. He wants to **meet every need** of our lives.

My God shall supply all your need according to His riches in glory by Christ Jesus (Phil 4:19).

God says, "Just ask Me, and it will be given."

Chapter Two

WHEN DOES GOD ANSWER PRAYER?

And it came to pass, as He was praying in a certain place, when He ceased, that one of His disciples said to Him "Lord, teach us to pray, as John also taught his disciples." So He said to them, "When you pray, say:

Our Father in heaven, Hallowed be Your name. Your kingdom come. Your will be done On earth as it is in heaven. Give us day by day our daily bread. And forgive us our sins, For we also forgive everyone who is indebted to us. And do not lead us into temptation, But deliver us from the evil one."

And He said to them, "Which of you shall have a friend, and go to him at midnight and say to him, 'Friend, lend me three loaves; for a friend of mine has come to me on his journey, and I have nothing to set before him'; and he will answer from within and say, 'Do not trouble me; the door is now shut, and my children are with me in bed; I cannot rise and give to you'? I say to you, though he will not rise and give to him because he is his friend, yet because of his persistence he will rise and give him as many as he needs. And I say to you, ask, and it will be given to you; seek, and you will find; knock, and it will be opened to you. For everyone who asks receives, and he who seeks finds, and to him who knocks it will be opened. If a son asks for bread from any father among you, will he give him a stone? Or if he asks for a fish, will he give him a serpent instead of a fish? Or if he asks for an egg, will he offer him a scorpion? If you then, being evil, know how to give good gifts to your children, how much more will your heavenly Father give the Holy Spirit to those who ask Him!" (Lk. 11:1-13).

R. A. Torrey, one of the greatest Bible teachers to live on this continent, was very influential in the Bible Institute of Los Angeles which later became Biola University. He commented on why God used D. L. Moody who was not a well-educated man. He was not well-trained nor eloquent. He did not seem to have a lot of social grace, but he was mightily used by God. D. L. Moody was a friend of R. A. Torrey and he died in 1899. Torrey wrote these words about him:

There was a reason that D. L. Moody was used so mightily of God, and I was one of his closest friends, I saw his defects. I observed him up close, and I say without reservation that D. L. Moody gave himself wholly, unreservedly and unqualifiedly, entirely to God. The reason for the great power on Mr. Moody's life was that Moody was in the deepest and most meaningful sense, a man of prayer. I knew him well. Many people remember Moody primarily as a great preacher. He preached to more people than all of previous history had ever recorded.

According to Dr. Torrey, he was a far greater pray-er than a preacher. His prayers were not marked by any theological sophistication. They were simple, trustful, definite, direct, persistent in their intercession and seemed often like a child was praying.

Moody, himself, said, "I would rather be able to pray like David, than to preach with the eloquence of Gabriel." Perhaps no man in U. S. history was faced with such great problems financially and administratively—challenges that seemed insurmountable, things that people said could never be done. Yet when Moody was confronted with these large scale problems, he still believed that nothing was impossible with God. He would always call a few friends together to pray.

Torrey died a long time ago, but he wrote, "I wonder how many ministries in America would be absolutely revolutionized by God if they just knew one thing that Moody knew—God answers prayer."

The founder of Biola, the Rev. Thomas C. Horton wrote a book on prayer called, "The Potency of Prayer". Biola was founded in 1908 and the book is really old. T. C. Horton told how the founding of Biola was bathed in prayer.

"It has pleased God to put in His Holy Word in plain, definite terms, the meaning, the purpose, and the power of prayer and to give the fullest assurance that His desire is to hear the requests and supply the needs of His own. If there could but come to the church a revival of real prayer in which the whole body of believers would unite, there would surely come, not merely showers of blessing, but the abundant rain that would refresh the souls of saints, revolutionize the church, and make glad the heart of the Lord who gave His life for fallen man."

John Hyde was known not only as a great missionary to India, but also as "Praying Hyde". A classmate said of him:

He did not excel as a student, though he might have been above average, and when he went to India as a missionary most people did not think he would make it. He gave no promise of being the remarkable missionary he turned out to be. He lacked enthusiasm. He lacked zeal, which everybody said a young missionary pioneering in the country of India would need. A mighty change took place in John Hyde's life when he learned on the mission field, that there was only one thing that really worked. That was prayer. Within a few short years, thousands of people came to know Christ through this man who became known as "The Apostle of Prayer". The work of winning people to Christ became a passion in his life and he said that it came on his knees. Shaking with sobs many times as he prayed, friends would hear him cry, "Oh God, give me souls or I die!" The more he prayed, the greater became his passion for souls, the greater the numbers of the people of India that were won to Christ. If only the church today could grasp the meaning of prayer in God's program and be willing to pay the price!"

There's one thing that God blesses more than anything else—prayer! We need to know when He will answer!

WHEN WE PRAY IN JESUS' NAME

There is no question that so grieves the hearts of the children of God as, "Why doesn't God answer my prayer?" Many people tell me that they have been praying for something for a long time and nothing has happened. Why? "Why hasn't God answered my prayer?"

The first thing to consider is that God answers our prayers when we pray in Jesus name. We're not talking about tacking those words on the end of our prayers. That is proper and should be done. We should say, "In the name of our Lord Jesus Christ, Amen." However, we are not talking simply about the title "Jesus Christ our Lord". We have something far more significant even than that! We're talking about the application of who He is. When we pray in Jesus' name, God says He answers prayer.

"Whatever you ask in My name, that I will do, that the Father may be glorified in the Son. If you ask anything in My name, I will do it" (Jn. 14:13-14).

Apparently, praying in Jesus' name is to pray in order that God the Father be glorified. It's interesting that you trace this in the immediate context leading up to John 14. In John 12:23 Jesus said, *"The hour has come that the Son of Man should be glorified."* Now look at John 13:26. As they gathered around for the Last Supper, the Passover, I read that Jesus said, *"It is he to whom I shall give a piece of bread when I have dipped it."*

And having dipped the bread, He gave it to Judas Iscariot, the son of Simon. Now after the piece of bread, Satan entered him. Then Jesus said to him, "What you do, do quickly." But no one at the table knew for what reason He said this to him. For some thought, because Judas had the money box, that Jesus had said to him, "Buy those things we need for the feast," or that he should give something to the poor. Having received the piece of bread, he then went out immediately. And it was night. So when he had gone out, Jesus said, "Now the Son of Man is glorified, and God is glorified in Him. If God is glorified in Him, God will also glorify Him in Himself, and glorify Him immediately."

"You did not choose Me, but I chose you and appointed you that you should go and bear fruit, and that your fruit should remain that whatever you ask the Father in My name He may give you" (Jn. 15:16).

"And in that day you will ask Me nothing. Most assuredly, I say to you, whatever you ask the Father in My name He will give you. Until now you have asked nothing in My name. Ask, and you will receive, that your joy may be full" (Jn. 16:23- 24).

Jesus spoke these words, lifted up His eyes to heaven, and said: "Father, the hour has come, Glorify Your Son, that Your Son also may glorify You, as You have given Him authority over all flesh, that He should give eternal life to as many as You have given Him. And this is eternal life, that they may know You, the only true God, and Jesus Christ whom You have sent. I have glorified You on the earth. I have finished the work which You have given me to do. And now, O Father, glorify me together with Yourself, with the glory which I had with You before the world was" (Jn. 17:1-5).

Now look again at John 14 with new eyesight. It says, *" ... whatever you ask in My name, that I will do, that the Father may be glorified in the Son."* If you follow the thought, Jesus Himself said that the hour is going to come when God is going to be glorified and God is going to glorify Jesus. At the time of the Last Supper when Judas went out, after he left, Jesus said, *"Now the Son of Man is glorified, and God is glorified in Him."* Why were they being *"glorified"* just then? Because prophecy was being fulfilled.

The prophecy about *"the hand that is with me at the table, will betray Me"* from the Old Testament was being fulfilled. The time of Jesus' death was at hand and he said that was the time when God was going to glorify Him. All through this text, as you read it and see the context, you begin to see what prayer in the name of Jesus Christ really is! **It is praying that God would be glorified!**

God was glorified through all the events of the trial and the suffering, and the death of our Lord Jesus Christ.

When we pray IN JESUS' NAME, we are giving glory to God because we, in fact, are trusting what God has done to bring glory to Himself.

Let me put it another way—most praying is not in Jesus' name because the **motive** is really to glorify man, not God. Sometimes even a GOOD THING does not seek to glorify God. God is to be glorified in all things and Jesus said that when we ask in His name, the Father will be glorified.

IN MY NAME is more than just a title. It is referring to the whole ministry and work and authority of Jesus Christ. Does your prayer center in the purpose of Jesus Christ who came to seek and to save that which was lost? Does what you're asking God to do, whatever it is, accomplish the purposes of God? Or is it something you want God to do in your life simply because you want it done.

This is a very serious matter. When we pray in the name of Jesus, in His authority, after His mission and purpose, then God will be glorified. All through the death, the suffering, the trial and the betrayal, God's purpose is being honored. Prophecy is being fulfilled. This is a constant theme through this text. When we pray in Jesus' name, we're saying, "God, YOU be glorified! YOUR purposes which may be unknown to me, be fulfilled in my life and the lives of those for whom I am praying!"

WHEN WE PRAY ACCORDING TO HIS WILL

> *Now this is the confidence that we have in Him, that if we ask anything according to His will, He hears us. And if we know that He hears us, whatever we ask, we know that we have the petitions we have asked of Him* (I Jn. 5:14-15).

Many people think this is just like the previous point in John 14. There is a specific here that will help us. It is automatic that God hears our prayers. After all, He hears everything that anyone says! There's not an idle word that He doesn't know about. So, can we say that God answers everyone's prayer? The answer is, "No! Absolutely not!"

Some people find comfort in saying that God answers "Yes", "No", and "Maybe". But I want you to know that the Bible teaches that God **isn't answering** the prayers of the wicked, for instance. We'd better wake up and see in the Bible, the many reasons why God isn't answering prayer. Don't think that God is some great "puppet in the sky" and if you pull the right strings, He will do what you want. God will answer prayer when we pray according to His will!

Whatever we ask *"according to His will, He hears ...."* I didn't just say, He listens—He hears! The idea is to hearken to it and answer, doing something about it. You could say, "If we ask anything according to His will, He ANSWERS us." We're not just talking about Someone who hears us because He hears all things. We're talking about Someone who ANSWERS our requests. He hearkens to ANYBODY who prays ACCORDING TO HIS WILL.

Now you have this assurance, if you can line your prayer up with what the will of God is, you have automatic answers! That's pretty good, isn't it?

Verse 15 goes on to say, *"If we know that He hears us, whatever we ask, we know that we have the petitions we have asked of Him."* How does a person speak confidently, "I KNOW that what I asked of the Lord will happen"? We can say this when we ask ACCORDING TO HIS WILL.

Be careful! Sometimes we're tempted to tack it onto the end of our prayer, just to be sure we got it in. "Lord, I want You to do this ... if it be Your will." We're almost afraid NOT to say it for fear of getting zapped right on the spot! We reassure the Lord that **whatever** we've prayed, we really want His will to be done. We seem to think that we "need" a Ferrari, or we shouldn't have to work for minimum wage because we're the King's kids! I don't read that in the Bible! Maybe that is what God wants for you! Pray according to His will.

You tell me, where is there an accurate expression of God's will? In the Bible, of course. How many times do we check this Book when we're praying about something? That's where we'll find out if what we're asking is really the will of God! Perhaps we're confused by God's grace in answering many of our prayers when they, in fact, can't be proven to be in His will. Perhaps you're praying for a hundred dollars this week. There's no verse that tells you He will give you a hundred dollars this week. How can you say that's "the will of God"? Yet, God often does that! He gives someone a hundred dollars just when they need it, and He doesn't have to do it!

One friend of mine says, "God does this to mess your brain up!" It is so that you never think you know what God is going to do. God is in charge! One thing for sure, though, if you want God to answer your prayer, line it up with what God's will is. There are things of God in the Bible that are clearly the will of God. They are known as His will—called that in His word.

There is a great story about the will of God in D.L. Moody's life. He had three children and his son, Will, was in total rebellion. It was Moody's greatest grief and he wondered what he had done wrong. The child rebelled against all his father stood for although he was a brillant young man and became a doctor. Moody bore that grief but he never stopped praying for his boy. For years, his son was totally rebellious and far from God. Sometimes, Moody couldn't even get up to preach because he knew his son was completely away from God. Moody's associates knew he'd trained him in the Word of God and he loved his son, but when the boy had been in school and away from home, he'd gotten his mind messed up and would have nothing to do with the Bible.

Moody had the encouragement of the Word of God to know what God's will was and, when anyone asked him about it, he said that He knew that God would be faithful to His promises. As time proved God's faithfulness, the son came to the Lord with his whole heart, and he became very active in the ministry of D. L. Moody. He became a giant for God in Moody's ministry. All along, Moody had confidence that God would answer prayer! God was faithful to His will which is that no one *"should perish but that all should come to repentance"* (II Peter 3:9).

WHEN WE PRAY WITH FAITH

Now in the morning, as they passed by, they saw the fig tree dried up from the roots. And Peter, remembering, said to Him, "Rabbi, look! The fig tree which You cursed has withered away." So Jesus answered and said to them, "Have faith in God. For assuredly, I say to you, whoever says to this mountain, 'Be removed and be cast into the sea,' and does not doubt in his heart, but believes that those things he says will come to pass, he will have whatever he says. Therefore I say to you, whatever things you ask when you pray, believe that you receive them, and you will have them" (Mk. 11:20- 24).

How do you like that? Could it be that some of these "wacko" preachers aren't so bad after all? They've been saying, "You pray for it and you can have it!" I listened to a guy on TV not long ago and he made me mad with his "Name it! Claim it!" preaching. God answers prayer when we pray with faith, but **we don't set aside** praying in Jesus' name; **we don't set aside** praying according to His will; **we don't set aside** that the faith is not in ourselves and our ability to believe, but in God!

There is a subtle influence in our culture that somehow, people with great faith are being honored by God by having their prayers answered! I don't see that in the Bible at all! In fact, all the examples in the Bible tell us that most of us don't have much faith at all. We're talking little faith. Jesus said, "You guys don't have much faith, but even if it's only as much as a tiny mustard seed, you can do better than you're doing now!"

The centurion said, *"Lord, I believe! Help Thou mine unbelief!"* Where are these great believers in our midst? I don't read that **great faith is honored** by God. I read that **God honors faith in a great God!**

Jesus never said that we should have faith in **our ability to believe God.** He said, *"Have faith in God!"* He who made the mountain, can remove it. If you believe it, pray in the name of Jesus, asking for His will, a mountain could literally be moved by God. He made the mountain; He can move it if He wants to. It is critical that we believe God. When we pray with faith, God will answer prayer.

> *But without faith it is impossible to please Him, for he who comes to God must believe that He is, and that He is a rewarder of those who diligently seek Him* (Heb. 11:6).

It is **the character of God** that we believe. It is **the power of God** that we believe. We don't believe in our ability to believe, but we believe in Him—**His** power, **His** faithfulness, **His** character.

Whether we like it or not, we cannot fool God. You could say to your friend that you believe something is going to happen, but if you don't really believe it in your heart, God knows it. It's interesting how often we pray for something, but we don't really believe it's going to happen. We can kid ourselves, and fool our friends. We can pray for rain, and carry an umbrella today, but if it doesn't rain today, we probably won't have the nerve to carry the umbrella tomorrow! It isn't some act of ours that demonstrates that we really believe.

If you come to God, and you believe in who He is, and that He is *"the rewarder of those who diligently seek Him"*, that's one thing. However, if you think that answers to prayer depend on your ability to believe it, or to claim it (or to demand it), you're going to be sadly mistaken in life.

When we pray, we pray with faith, but not faith in ourselves or our ability to believe. We pray with **faith in God**.

There is a passage that gives us an analysis of this matter. It deals with wisdom and we know that God wants us to be wise; that is His will. When you ask God for wisdom, you're asking for the right thing. Does God answer that prayer? Yes! If we need wisdom in the body of Christ, it is proper to ask God for wisdom. God says that's right on target! God says He'll give it to us, and never criticize us for asking for wisdom. You'd think that would make us ask for it more often!

> *But let him ask in faith, with no doubting, for he who doubts is like a wave of the sea driven and tossed by the wind. For let not that man suppose that he will receive anything from the Lord; he is a double-minded man, unstable in all his ways* (James 1:6-8).

This may be one reason we don't get the answers to our prayers that we are looking for—we are harboring doubts! Here the word *"double-minded man"* means a *"double-souled man"*. He's going in two directions at the same time. He's saying one thing with his mouth, but his heart is going another way. A man who says he's asking in faith, but yet is doubting in that way, is divided. The word "doubt", means divided. It separates (divides) **what God can do** from **what I see** in my circumstances. There are a lot of us who do not see any answers in our circumstances so we really don't believe in God although we continue to pray.

Prayer can become a routine, mechanical thing. If your circumstances and events as you know them, are now controlling your perspective of prayer, your heart is going in the direction of **not** believing. Then, if you **say that you believe** God can answer prayer, you are being hypocritical. That is going in two directions! That man won't get anything from God, James says.

God is honored when we, in a sense, are so stupid that we believe He can do it when our circumstances give no sign of change. We need to believe that He can actually do it. When we pray with faith, God says He will answer.

WHEN WE ABIDE IN HIM AND HIS WORDS ABIDE IN US

"If you abide in Me, and My words abide in you, you will ask what you desire, and it shall be done for you. By this My Father is glorified, that you bear much fruit; so you will be My disciples" (Jn. 15:7-8).

I'd like to point out that this is still in the context of our first point—how God is glorified. Jesus said we would get what we ask for so that God will be glorified. Here is the same thing! We can ask whatever we want!

What's needed of us here? What is *"abiding in Him"*? Is He talking about non-Christians? What does it mean for His words to abide in us? It means that the Word of God, what Jesus taught us, is now making its home in our lives. Our thoughts, our desires, our volitional choices are being dominated and governed by the Word of God. Is God's Word governing your life? Is it at home in you?

If we are *"abiding in Christ"*, we are comfortable with the Lord Jesus. Is he your best Friend? Or do you sometimes try to be a "secret service" Christian? Why are we so uncomfortable with our Lord Jesus Christ? He's King of kings and Lord of lords! Jesus said that we must not be ashamed of Him and His words. Paul said, *"I am not ashamed of the gospel of Christ for it is the power of God unto salvation to everyone who believes, to the Jew first and also to the Greek"* (Rom. 1:16).

Do you shrink back from who He is and what His Word says? Jesus said that if we make our home in Him, if we are comfortable with Him, we can ask whatever we desire and He will do it! Talk about "friend to friend"! What a relationship with God!

WHEN WE PRAY WITH HUMILITY

> *If My people who are called by My name will humble themselves, and pray and seek My face, and turn from their wicked ways, then I will hear from heaven, and will forgive their sin and heal their land* (II Chron. 7:14).

This is most important. God answers prayer when we pray with humility. God has promised to answer the prayers of those who humble themselves in His sight. Jesus gave us a parable on prayer regarding humility.

> *Also he spoke this parable to some who trusted in themselves that they were righteous, and despised others: "Two men went up to the temple to pray, one*

a Pharisee and the other a tax collector. The Pharisee stood and prayed thus with himself, 'God, I thank you that I am not like other men-extortioners, unjust, adulterers, or even as this tax collector. I fast twice a week; I give tithes of all that I possess.' And the the tax collector, standing afar off, would not so much as raise his eyes to heaven, but beat his breast, saying, 'God be merciful to me a sinner!' I tell you, this man went down to his house justified rather than the other; for everyone who exalts himself will be abased, and he who humbles himself will be exalted" (Lk. 18:9-14).

If your attitude is that you are righteous and you despise and look down on others, you can forget about being powerful in prayer! Who is going to be blessed by God? Whose prayer is going to be answered? It will be the one who prays with humility. Humble yourself in the sight of the Lord and He will lift you up.

Therefore submit to God. Resist the devil and he will flee from you. Draw near to God and He will draw near to you. Cleanse your hands, you sinners; and purify your hearts, you double-minded. Lament and mourn and weep! Let your laughter be turned to mourning and your joy to gloom. Humble yourselves in the sight of the Lord, and He will lift you up (James 4:7-10).

We could talk for a long time about humility and still not grasp it all. That's for sure! Humility is a lesson that is never learned. Did you ever think about that? The moment you think you've mastered what the Bible says about humility, in that moment you are tempted to be proud about what you know about humility. You can be proud that you are humble! Do you understand that?

There are always people in the body of Christ who think they are commissioned of God to point out those who are not humble. There's enough in the hand of our Sovereign God to make us humble without any help from people! God will see to it that we either humble ourselves, or He will do it for us! When we pray, it MUST BE with humility.

One writer says about this parable, when we pray with humility, we beat our breasts as the penitent sinner did and realize that there is not an ounce of worthiness in us as to why God should answer our prayers. It should be a miracle to our hearts that God answers any of our prayers! We ought to be grateful from the bottom of our hearts for any little display of God's sovereign power used to answer a prayer of ours! Imagine it! Sinners that we are, why should God answer our prayers? Who do we think we are!

Pray with humility, God says. Humble yourself and God will lift you up.

WHEN WE ARE OBEDIENT TO HIS WORD

One who turns away his ear from hearing the law, Even his prayer shall be an abomination (Prov. 28:9).

If you are disobedient to God's Word, your prayer is an ABOMINATION to Him! You turn your heart away from what God says and your prayer turns into an abomination.

And whatever we ask we receive from Him, because we keep His commandments and do those things that are pleasing in His sight (I Jn. 3:22).

It seems to me, if I'm reading that verse correctly, that God really wants to answer our prayers! He really does! If I please Him, He really WANTS to answer my prayer. God is delighted in answering that prayer when we are obedient to His Word.

WHENEVER HE WANTS TO DO IT

This is the final answer to our question, "When does God answer prayer?" I don't hear this answer very often, but it's true! You've got to get a little bit of the sovereignty of God into your heart to understand this.

But our God is in heaven; He does whatever He pleases (Ps. 115:3).

Jesus said, "Here's how you pray - Our Father in heaven, Hallowed [sovereign] be Your name. Your kingdom come. YOUR WILL BE DONE ON EARTH AS IT IS IN HEAVEN."

Wait a minute! We didn't ask Him for anything! It doesn't matter—He's going to do what He wants to do anyway! We just need to **thank** Him for whatever He is doing in our lives. It sounds frivolous to us to say, "Thank you, Lord, for that flat tire and making me late for work today." I don't mean to be foolish, but the Bible does say, *"In everything give thanks; for this is the will of God in Christ Jesus for you"* (I Thess. 5:18).

It's funny how we can read those words then not apply them to our daily lives. The Bible says that God does whatever He pleases.

> *For I know that the Lord is great, And our Lord is above all gods. Whatever the Lord pleases He does, In heaven and in earth, In the seas and in all deep places* (Ps. 135:5-6).

He does whatever He wants to do! Let me ask you a question. Do you think that God has done what He wants to do in your life so far?

I heard a guy on the radio preaching about trusting God to do great things in your life. We are always hoping that we can do something wonderful ... tomorrow. We want God to do something great in our lives next week. But what about up to now? Has God done what He wanted to do in your life so far? It depends a lot on whether you are thinking of things in category "Good" or category "Bad". God will answer prayer in the strangest way sometimes.

I was called to a hospital where a man was dying several years ago. The family said, "David, don't tell him he's dying of cancer. We know you and you just don't hold back, but don't tell him." When I asked why, they said it might cause him to have a heart attack and die! He was dying anyway; who cared if he died of cancer or of a heart attack? Maybe I don't sound too compassionate, but I went in and the man really was ready to die. I called him by name and he grabbed my shirt and pulled me near and said, "David, am I dying of cancer?" In spite of the looks on their faces, I said, "Yes." "I knew it," he said. "I don't want to grieve my family. Have a word of prayer and ask the Lord to take me home." I suggested that we want to do God's will even in our last days. "I know that! Just pray that I will die and go home to be with the Lord." Has anyone ever asked you to do that? I didn't know what to do. His daughter said, "We know God can heal him." The man just shook his head. God could have healed him, we believe that, but he wanted to go home to heaven. So, I prayed and said, "Lord, I don't know what to do here. He wants me to pray that he come home to be with You. I know that's a great thing, so if You want to take him, take Him right now." The family gasped. The man died right on the spot. It scared me! I'll never forget what the doctor said! He never wanted me to pray for him!

Those people's kids are older now and they are friends, and we all kind of laugh about it now, but isn't that interesting? I just happened to be an instrument. God knew what He was going to do. He moved me in there, and said pray, but He already knew what He was going to do. Also, the man had the opinion that if God wanted to do it, he wanted it to be done. So, when I prayed in line with God's will, God took him! I still haven't quite recovered from it and that was over twenty years ago!

God will do whatever He wants to do ... WHATEVER HE WANTS TO DO! Do you believe that? It should affect our prayer life.

There are a lot of things in our lives we don't want. Also, there are a lot of things we want, and we don't know if God is going to give them to us or not. Sometimes we feel strange, even when we pray. We need to line up more and more with God's glory and His will and His Word.

Let's seek to glorify Him in all that we say and do so that when we pray, it is God that we want to honor and praise.

Let's look at prayer as a daily communication with God, talking to Him about everything.

Let's praise Him and thank Him for all that He does.

Let's remember that God **does** answer prayer.

Chapter Three

WHAT RESULTS CAN WE EXPECT?

And whatever you ask in My name, that I will do, that the Father may be glorified in the Son. If you ask anything in My name, I will do it (Jn. 14:13-14).

If you abide in Me, and My words abide in you, you will ask what you desire, and it shall be done for you (Jn. 15:7).

Until now you have asked nothing in My name. Ask, and you will receive, that your joy may be full (Jn. 16:24).

Ask, and it will be given to you; seek, and you will find; knock, and it will be opened to you. For everyone who asks receives, and he who seeks finds, and to him who knocks it will be opened (Matt. 7:7).

And when they had come to the multitude, a man came to Him, kneeling down to Him and saying, "Lord, have mercy on my son, for he is an epileptic and suffers severely; for he often falls into the fire and often into the water. So I brought him to Your disciples, but they could not cure him." Then Jesus answered and said, "O faithless and perverse generation, how long shall I be with you? How long shall I bear with you? Bring him here to Me." And Jesus rebuked the demon, and he came out of him; and the child was cured from that very hour. Then the disciples came to Jesus privately and said, "Why could we not cast him out?" So Jesus said to them, "Because of your unbelief; for assuredly, I say to you, if you have faith as a mustard seed, you will say to this mountain, 'Move from here to there,' and it will move; and nothing will be impossible for you. However, this kind does not go out except by prayer and fasting" (Matt. 17:14-21).

Now in the morning, as He returned to the city, He was hungry. And seeing a fig tree by the road, He came to it and found nothing on it but leaves, and said to it, "Let no fruit grow on you ever again." And immediately the fig tree withered away. Now when the disciples saw it, they marveled, saying, "How did the fig tree wither away so soon?" So Jesus answered and said to them, "Assuredly I say to you, if you have faith and do not doubt, you will not only do what was done to the fig tree, but also if you say to this mountain, 'Be removed and be cast into the sea,' it will be done. And all things, whatever you ask in prayer, believing, you will receive" (Matt. 21:18-22).

"And I say to you, ask, and it will be given to you; seek, and you will find; knock, and it will be opened to you. For everyone who asks receives, and he who seeks finds, and to him who knocks it will be opened. If a son asks for bread from any father

among you, will he give him a stone? Or if he asks for a fish, will he give him a serpent instead of a fish? Or if he asks for an egg, will he offer him a scorpion? If you then, being evil, know how to give good gifts to your children, HOW MUCH MORE will your heavenly Father give the Holy Spirit to those who ask Him!" (Lk. 11:9)

PEACE OF MIND AND HEART

Be anxious for nothing, but in everything by prayer and supplication, with thanksgiving, let your requests be made known to God; and the peace of God, which surpasses all understanding, will guard your hearts and minds through Christ Jesus (Phil. 4:6-7).

Not a week goes by but that there is something in our lives about which we could be troubled. What should we do? James 5:13 says that if anyone is *"suffering* (that is emotional suffering), *let him pray."* Let's suppose you're troubled about something; the Bible says to pray about it. Peace of mind and heart is a promised result of prayer.

You will keep him in perfect peace, Whose mind is stayed on You, Because he trusts in You (Isaiah 26:3).

"Be anxious for nothing, but in everything by prayer and supplication, with thanksgiving, let your requests be made known to God; and the peace of God which surpasses all understanding, will guard your hearts and minds through Christ Jesus" (Phil. 4:6-7).

It does NOT go on to say, "Don't expect God to do anything about it!"

It DOES go on to say that you will have peace and you won't be able to figure it out. What is the result of prayer? One of the first things is peace of mind.

There are a thousand things to take our minds off the Lord, and we need to have peace. I want you to analyze Philippians 4:6-7 and find out why you don't get peace when you pray. Maybe you've been praying and you still don't have peace of heart and mind. Let's look at these verses.

"Be anxious for nothing." The word *"anxious"* is a Greek word meaning *"to divide"*. Do you remember when Jesus was at the home of Mary and Martha (Lk. 10:38-42)? Jesus said, "Martha, Martha, you are distracted about many things! Mary has chosen that good part." Jesus said that Mary, who was sitting at His feet to learn from Him, was choosing the best part. He indicated that He appreciated Martha's service but that she was all messed up and troubled because Mary wasn't helping. The words *"troubled"*, *"worried"*, *"distracted"* are the same word we find in Philippians 4:6-7—*"anxious"*. *"Be anxious for nothing."*

The Greek word is *"to divide"* and it means instead of focussing on the Lord and what He can do, you're looking at the circumstances, or the problem, or the emotional turmoil you're in and that dominates your heart. Jesus isn't dominant, nor what He can do. In fact, you're not asking Jesus to do anything. You are *"troubled"* about everything that is happening.

The circumstances of life, on any given day, can wipe out the best of us. Do you believe that? God can overwhelm us any day; He can show us that we need His peace. Peace is the result of not losing your focus, keeping your mind and heart centered on the Lord and what He can do.

Don't be *"divided"* about anything. You say that I don't know your problem. True! But no matter how serious it is, focus on the Lord.

It's also possible that you did not do what the verse says, *" ... with thanksgiving ...."* I don't know about you, but I find it hard to say "Thank you" for that which is category "Bad". I have trouble saying things like, "Thank you, Lord. I cut my finger and now I've got my hand in a cast." It's amazing how many things in life are troublesome and we can't figure out why they happen. We just don't understand. God says, "Don't be distracted!"

I've almost come to the conclusion that we're not going to understand anything until we get to heaven. There are so many things that happen in life that we can't figure out. Why in the world do all these things happen to us? *"Be anxious for nothing."* Yet, a lot of us are into that—we are anxious.

> *"Therefore I say to you, DO NOT WORRY about your life, what you will eat or what you will put on. Is not life more than food and the body more than clothing? Look at the birds of the air, for they neither sow nor reap nor gather into barns; yet your heavenly Father feeds them. Are you not of much more value than they? Which of you by worrying can add one cubit to his stature? So why do you*

worry about clothing? Consider the lilies of the field, how they grow: they neither toil nor spin; and yet I say to you that even Solomon in all his glory was not arrayed like one of these. Now if God so clothes the grass of the field, which today is, and tomorrow is thrown into the oven, will He not much more clothe you, O you of little faith? Therefore, DO NOT WORRY, saying 'What shall we eat?' or 'What shall we drink?' or 'What shall we wear?' For after all these things the Gentiles seek. For your heavenly Father knows that you need all these things. But seek first the kingdom of God and His righteousness, and all these things shall be added to you. Therefore DO NOT WORRY ABOUT TOMOR-ROW, for tomorrow will worry about its own things. Sufficient for the day is its own trouble" (Matt. 6:25-34).

That means that there is so much hassle tomorrow that, if God let you in on it in advance, it would wipe you out. Why even bother thinking about it? We don't know anything about what will happen tomorrow so how can we know what we ought to worry about? You think you know what you'll be doing tomorrow, but you don't know anything for sure. Things could change tomorrow and be different than any other day you've ever lived. Maybe your wife usually serves you breakfast, but tomorrow she may get angry and not serve you anything! *"Be anxious for NOTHING!"*

Do you have a list of things you worry about? Don't do it! It says *"...for nothing"*! I'll tell you what to do if you're really troubled—make a list, numbering all the things you are worrying about. "I didn't get paid this week." "I had a flat tire." "My wife yelled at me." "I yelled back." Make a list! Now, look at it and realize that God said, *"Be anxious for nothing!"* Then tear up the list. God said not to think a thing about it.

One of the wonderful results of prayer is peace of mind and heart. God has promised to *"keep"* your heart and mind through Jesus Christ.

FULLNESS OF JOY

"Until now you have asked nothing in My name. Ask, and you will receive, that your joy may be full" (Jn.16:24).

Why should we pray? What results can we expect? We can expect FULLNESS OF JOY! If you want to stop being happy, just stop praying! That's real easy to do. Just stop talking to the Lord about things and take all the burden yourself. Don't once think about giving it to the Lord. Talk about the strength you need to carry the load, and tell everybody that you're capable and can handle it. Don't consider prayer at all. That's a good way to be unhappy!

If you want fullness of joy even when things are going bad, then pray! Take your burdens to the Lord ... and be sure to keep them after you've talked to Him. Is that what it says? You've got to dump them on Him! *"Cast your burden on the Lord, and He will sustain you,"* says Isaiah 55.

I Peter 5:7 says, *"Cast all your care upon Him."* Once again, we find that word for *"anxious"*—*"Cast all your anxieties on Him, for He cares for you."* He'll take care of it. Don't worry about it! Fullness of joy is a by-product of consistent prayer. There will be joy in your heart when you see what God can do.

DIVINE HEALING

It's amazing how many folks ask me if I believe in healing. Of course I do! Don't you? First of all, I believe very strongly in the best healing you can ever have—the resurrection of your body! That's what I call real healing! We're talking here about permanent, ultimate healing. The very best healing you could possibly have is the resurrection when the Lord comes again.

Everything between now and your death (or the Lord's return) is kind of a troublesome deal. You ask, "Can the Lord heal me?"

Can He heal you of a bad spirit? Sure. Can He heal you of a sick mind? Yes. Can He heal you of a drug habit? Absolutely! Can He heal you of alcoholism? Yes. Can the Lord heal a sore that's on your body? People say, "In time."

Have you noticed how people vacillate about healing? Suppose it doesn't happen when you pray for it. What is the next step? "You didn't have enough faith," they tell us. That's interesting to me because Jesus healed people that didn't even believe in Him. Evidently, it's not necessary! A lot of us think that it is, though, so we go through some trauma because someone else got healed and we didn't.

There's also an assumption that somehow healing is better than sickness. I haven't found that in the Bible although I've been trying to look at this fairly. I don't believe that you can prove that temporary healing (something that happens before the resurrection) is better than sickness. First of all, there are more good things said in the Bible about sickness and suffering than are said about healing. It seems that it might be better if we suffer a little. We learn a lot more! Much more blessing comes to us that way. Still, not many of us go into deep, earnest, fervent prayer over suffering. "Dear Lord, please bring me a ton of suffering tomorrow! Flood my body with illness and make me incapacitated. I don't even want to walk." Nobody prays like that! Nevertheless, there is a lot more blessing in suffering and sickness than in healing and it creates a little problem for us.

Does God heal everybody who is sick? Did you answer no? Yes, ultimately, He does. If you get sick and you die, the resurrection is going to heal you. So, God does ultimately heal every believer who is sick. I read a little book that said God wants everyone to be well. Somebody gave it to me and I read it. It didn't work for me, but I read it. I thought the writer could have saved a lot of time and just told us about the resurrection because that's when I would agree. God wants us so well that He's going to eliminate the problem that made us sick!

In this life now, does God heal anybody that's sick? Certainly! If you took some medicine and got better, did God heal you? If there are any properties in the medicine that came out of anything on the planet, who do you think made it? God did!

Let's suppose a surgeon helped you. I had a big gash in my hand and a surgeon sewed it up, and it's gone now. Did the surgeon heal me, or did God heal me? The surgeon sewed me up. I had a little fun with the doctor. I went for my final check-up and put the other hand out for him to look at. I couldn't resist. "It's a miracle!" he said. Then I put out the hand that had been cut.

When God heals you, does He only heal the things that nobody sees? Doesn't it bother you that broken bones, sticking out through the skin, aren't immediately put back together? Why is the healing that people claim so hard to verify? I believe that God can heal, and I believe that God does a good job when He heals.

One person told me that God healed her by putting a filling in her tooth. She insisted even though it didn't look like a real good job to me. I thought to myself, "God couldn't have done that! God doesn't do bad dentistry!" Why would God put in a filling? Wouldn't He give you a brand new tooth? Come on! Let's be serious about healing. If God heals you, does He do a partial job?

If I were God, I would want to do it really well so that I'd get all the glory! Think with me! Do you believe that God, in this life, before the resurrection, can actually perform an instantaneous healing and restore your body as though nothing had ever happened?

> *Is anyone among you sick? Let him call for the elders of the church, and let them pray over him, anointing him with oil in the name of the Lord. And the prayer of faith will save the sick, and the Lord will raise him up. And if he has committed sins, he will be forgiven. Confess your trespasses to one another, and pray for one another, that you may be healed. The effective, fervent prayer of a righteous*

man avails much. Elijah was a man with a nature like ours, and he prayed earnestly that it would not rain; and it did not rain on the land for three years and six months. And he prayed again, and the heaven gave rain, and the earth produced its fruit. Brethren, if anyone among you wanders from the truth, and someone turns him back, let him know that he who turns a sinner from the error of his way will save a soul from death and cover a multitude of sins (James 5:14-20).

There are a lot of questions this passage brings up. What does *"sick"* mean? When you have the flu, do you call for the elders? If you have a cold, or a little sore, do you call them? The word *"sick"* in the Bible is used of Dorcas in Acts 9, and she died. It's used of Lazarus in John 11, and he died. It's used of the impotent man in John 5, who had no way to help himself and no one else could help him. We're talking about serious illness here.

The Greek word means *"without strength"* and it was used in ancient times of someone who had consulted doctors and was told there was nothing they could do. Are there illnesses like that in the body of Christ? You bet! Many, many times doctors have to fold their hands and say there is nothing left to do. We're talking about serious illness here when a believer is faced with illness beyond medical help. The Bible says, *"Let him call for the elders of the church."* God makes sure it's serious—that's why He used the word He used. He's not talking about the flu or a cold. God wants to make sure we know why He's going to do this and how His power will be displayed.

"Call for the elders of the church." Should I do that or at the end of a meeting, should I ask the sick people to come forward and be anointed? Is that what a pastor should do? The Greek word is *"to call to yourself";* it's a private meeting. It's not a public meeting. These safeguards are interesting! It's so that we won't be bragging or glorying in man's power.

"Let the sick person call to himself the elders"—plural! God doesn't want any one person to think they have power to heal. Only God heals! There are a lot of checks and balances here.

It says, *" ... let them pray ... ";* that is the elders, not the sick one. In the modern display of healing, it is the lack of faith in the person who isn't healed that is given as the reason for not being healed. The Bible says it is the elders who are to pray—not the sick person!

The elders are to *"pray over him, anointing him with oil"* so some people think the oil is therapeutic. Some think it is medicinal. I don't believe that. The word *"anointing"* is the sacred anointing when they poured the oil over the High Priest's garments to anoint him and dedicate him to the Lord. The word *"Christ"* is the same word—*"the Anointed One".* We are talking about a sacred symbol, emphasizing the power of God. It's the oil of the Holy Spirit's power, not a medicinal use of oil. According to the Bible, it is just symbolic, but it is an important symbol. It symbolizes the power of the Holy Spirit and what God can do.

"And the prayer of faith ... " it says. We're talking about results! Don't you want to pray that way? I sure do! The word for *"prayer"* is not the word for **"demand"**. Out of

the many words for prayer, this one is the simple word for worship, or give thanks. Literally, this word means to *"give thanks toward ..."*, meaning toward God.

It's a prayer of thanksgiving. It's a prayer of faith, not YOUR faith but a prayer of THE faith—the Greek has the definite article. It refers to the sum total of what God has revealed. It's a prayer that is in the light of the Word of God, in accordance with *"the faith that was once for all delivered to the saints"*.

It isn't MY ability to believe that heals anybody! It's God who heals. *"The Lord will raise him up."*

Then, it mentions sin because some people are blocking the power of God in their lives in regard to physical ailments because of sin—trespasses against brothers and sisters in Christ. If we would confess them and get right with the Lord, healing would come ... if sin is the problem. Many times, that is not the problem.

We're given an example of Elijah. He was a man like us—not a super-saint who could really believe God and had a special power on his life to do something spectacular. We're not talking about that at all! Even when the disciples were given the authority to cast out demons in the days of Jesus, they couldn't do it! Jesus said that the reason was that demons come out by prayer! They were not trusting God; they thought that, somehow, they had the power!

The ONLY one who performs healing is God! He's the one who heals. I look at this text and I see that Elijah was just like me and he prayed that it wouldn't rain, and it didn't rain for three years and six months. Then he prayed again, and it rained. You say that you're no Elijah! I'm not so sure! If you know the story, you know that Elijah wound up in a cave running away from Jezebel with God asking him why he was hiding!

God gave him a visible demonstration of his problem. He caused an earthquake, but God wasn't in the earthquake. He caused a lot of spectacular demonstrations of nature, but God wasn't in any of them. God was in a still, small voice and He told Elijah to get out of the cave. Here was a giant who called on God to answer prayer and changed the weather, but was not able to handle his own fears of Queen Jezebel!

He even felt sorry for himself! "I am the only one left of the servants of the Lord!" God said, "Get up and go do what I told you to do! By the way, I've got seven thousand others who haven't bowed the knee to Baal, either. You're not the only one. You can be replaced!" That was the basic message. That's true of all of us—we can be replaced. If you don't want to serve God, or if you want to get the glory yourself, then God will put you on the shelf and use somebody else! God's got a lot of spiritual giants out there!

What results can we expect? The Bible says we can be healed. God doesn't heal everybody. He does whatever He wants to do. Have you ever seen God heal anyone in answer to prayer? I have, and I have been the recipient of it myself. God heals, but He wants ALL the glory. You can expect God to work when you pray like He told you to pray.

So much prayer in our generation is self-oriented, is not rooted in God, and we *"ask amiss to consume it upon our own lusts"*. When we are simply trying to get something from God based on our own desires that have nothing to do with the glory of God, then I doubt seriously that we are going to get what we expect from God. God answers prayer, but we'd better do it His way!

OPEN DOORS FOR THE WORD OF GOD

Continue earnestly in prayer, being vigilant in it with thanksgiving; meanwhile praying also for us, that God would open to us a door for the word, to speak the mystery of Christ, for which I am also in chains (Col. 4:2-3).

I like what one missionary said when someone asked why the walls of Communism have fallen. Without hesitation he said, "It's because God's people have been praying for it for a long time." How interesting! It didn't happen at the diplomatic table. God is answering prayer! Do you believe God opens doors for His Word?

Is it hard to talk to the guy you work with? God answers prayer! He does! He opens doors for the Word of God.

Lydia, the seller of purple, was a wealthy lady of Thyatira living in the city of Philippi, and Paul met her down at the riverside. He shared the Word of God and it says that "the Lord opened her heart". God opens the doors of individual hearts and opens doors of opportunity for the Word. We need to pray that God would do that.

BOLDNESS IN PROCLAIMING THE GOSPEL

Praying always with all prayer and supplication in the Spirit, being watchful to this end with all

*perseverance and supplication for all the saints—
and for me, that utterance may be given to me, that I
may open my mouth boldly to make known the
mystery of the gospel, for which I am an ambassador
in chains that in it I may speak boldly, as I ought to
speak* (Eph. 6:18-20).

Are you having trouble sharing Christ with those on your
prayer list? Is it a family member, or somebody at work and
you want to share the gospel with them, but you can't be
bold? What's wrong? Prayer opens up that boldness. God
will give you boldness in proclaiming the gospel.

PROTECTION FROM WICKED MEN

*Finally, brethren, pray for us, that the word of
the Lord may have free course and be glorified, just
as it is with you, and that we may be delivered from
unreasonable and wicked men; for not all have faith.
But the Lord is faithful, who will establish you and
guard you from the evil one* (II Thess. 3:1-3).

Are you being hassled by wicked people? Are there
threats? Are there hostilities that you face? God answers
prayer and brings us protection from wicked men. Prayer is
essential for protection from wicked men.

WISDOM

*If any of you lacks wisdom, let him ask of God,
who gives to all liberally and without reproach, and
it will be given to him. But let him ask in faith, with*

no doubting, for he who doubts is like a wave of the sea driven and tossed by the wind. For let not that man suppose that he will receive anything from the Lord; he is a double-minded man, unstable in all his ways (James 1:5-8).

The little word *"if"* has many shades of expression in Greek grammar. This one is *"if ... and it is so"*! We would translate it **"***Since all of us lack wisdom, let us ask of God, who gives to all liberally and without reproach."*

I have seen God answer this prayer over and over and over again. *"If any of you lacks wisdom, let him ask of God."* I've seen wisdom being given by God in meetings where there was an absolute stalemate. Nobody understood what to do nor did they know the direction of the Lord. I've seen prayer answered whereby God gave wisdom and the whole problem was beautifully resolved. Everybody said, "How did that happen?"

There have been situations where people's minds were perplexed and no solution was to be found. Then, God gave wisdom in answer to prayer. How do you know you have wisdom when it operates? You always know you have wisdom when the application, the result, of what is discussed or said or done, brings glory to God and conforms to His Word. God's wisdom will bring the greatest amount of peace and order within relationships. When you have the wisdom of God, God's character will be honored and you will do what is right. When you have the wisdom of God, you will know exactly HOW to do things and you will get the greatest good from what you do.

The wisdom of God does more than any knowledge or learning we could ever do. God's wonderful wisdom is the ability to apply knowledge in a way that pleases the Lord, and glorifies Him, and honors Him. We need wisdom! God says, "Ask Me, and I'll give it to you."

I like the fact that He'll never jump on you for asking. Did you get that? You may have asked three times already this week, and you may think you're bugging God. The Bible says that God will continue to give you wisdom and will never reproach you for asking. He'll give it without criticizing you. He loves it when you ask Him!

When Solomon asked for wisdom, God gave him wisdom along with everything else that he DIDN'T ask for! God said that Solomon asked for the thing that pleased Him; he asked for a wise and discerning heart. Do you remember the story of the two women? Both were saying that the baby was theirs! I doubt seriously that many of us would ever apply the solution God gave Solomon in that instance. Solomon asked for a sword and laid the baby in his hand and offered to give each woman half of the baby! Just as he raised the sword, the real mother cried out, "No! Give the baby to her!" Then Solomon knew the real mother of that child. I love that story. God gave wisdom when Solomon asked.

SPIRITUAL POWER

Most of us are lacking in spiritual power. We don't experience it on a regular basis. It only comes as the result of prayer!

*For this reason I bow my knees to the Father of our Lord Jesus Christ, from whom the whole family in heaven and earth is named, that He would grant you, according to the riches of His glory, to be strengthened with might through His Spirit in the inner man, that Christ may dwell in your hearts through faith; that you, being rooted and grounded in love, may be able to comprehend with all the saints what is the width and length and depth and height—to know the love of Christ which passes knowledge; that you may be filled with all the fullness of God. Now to Him who is able to do exceedingly abundantly above all that we ask or think, **according to the power that works in us,** to Him be glory in the church by Christ Jesus throughout all ages, world without end. Amen. (Eph. 3:14-21).*

Spiritual power is the result of prayer.

A QUIET AND PEACEABLE LIFE IN SOCIETY

Therefore I exhort first of all that supplications, prayers, intercessions, and giving of thanks be made for all men, for kings and all who are in authority, that we may lead a quiet and peaceable life in all godliness and reverence (I Tim. 2:1-2).

A lot of people are concerned with what is going on in society. God says that prayer can do wonders. Do you see the news where they tell us about murder and rape and all that horrid stuff? We have a serious problem in our country.

There are crimes, disturbances and hostilities that hit us constantly. When I read this, I wonder if we're praying.

There was an issue in Congress and, from a biblical point of view, it was very clear what should be done. A group of us prayed that God would help our local congressmen to give the right biblical answer on that question. I'll tell you that my heart jumped with joy when I saw in the newspaper the list of how they voted. Every congressman in our area voted the right way! Do you wonder what "the right way" is? All you have to do is read the Bible and you'll find out what the right way is all the time! It's amazing!

I ran into one of our county supervisors and, even though I don't really know him, I walked up to him and said, "I want you to know that I'm praying for you that you will do what's right." He almost had a heart attack right on the spot! When he asked me why I was doing that, I told him that the Bible tells us that we ought to do this, so I was praying for him even though I didn't know much about him. He started to cry! He said that no one had ever said that to him before. I said, "Watch my lips! I'm praying for you."

It's amazing what God will do when we pray! It says that we should pray for political leaders so that *"we may lead a quiet and peaceable life in all godliness and reverence."*

HELP IN RESISTING TEMPTATION

"Watch and pray, lest you enter into temptation. The spirit indeed is willing, but the flesh is weak" (Matt. 26:41).

Jesus told us that we could expect help in resisting temptation if we would pray. *"Watch and pray."* Do you believe that by praying you can have victory over temptation? When folks are tempted, they usually don't think about praying! I said that to one young man who was having sex with his girlfriend and wanted to stop. I told him to pray the next time that he was in that situation. He said, "I wouldn't do that! That would kill it!" I told him that I thought that was the point!

"Watch and pray ... the spirit indeed is willing, but the flesh is weak." Is there some area that you're having trouble with? People are struggling with a lot of habits they wish they didn't have. Have you considered the power of prayer?

Do you believe God answers prayer? Do you believe that God can deliver you from drugs? Can he deliver you from the smoking habit you want to get rid of? The Bible doesn't say, "Thou shalt not smoke", but it's hurting you— it's damaging your lungs and your life! Most people I know want to quit. Do you have an alcohol problem? What is YOUR problem?

"Watch and pray that you enter not into temptation."

That's powerful! The enemy will not want you to pray when you're being tempted because God answers prayer.

LABORERS FOR THE HARVEST FIELDS OF THE WORLD

But when He saw the multitudes, He was moved with compassion for them, because they were weary and scattered, like sheep having no shepherd. Then

He said to His disciples, "The harvest truly is plenti-
ful, but the laborers are few. Therefore pray the
Lord of the harvest to send out laborers into His har-
vest."

And when He had called His twelve disciples to
Him, He gave them power ....

These twelve Jesus sent out (Matt. 9:36-38,
10:1,5).

One missionary writer says about this passage that you
have to be careful about praying for laborers for His harvest,
you may wind up going yourself! I like that.

How are we going to get more laborers for the harvest
fields of the world? God's answer is prayer! That's what it
says. *"PRAY the Lord of the harvest to send out laborers."*

THE SALVATION OF PEOPLE

Brethren, my heart's desire and prayer to God
for Israel is that they may be saved (Rom. 10:1).

A man asked me if the Bible says anywhere that you
should pray for the lost. Here it is! Do you have a list of
people you would like to see come to the Lord? Christians
often pray for family and friends who are lost and need the
Lord. What can we expect from God? We can expect to see
people find salvation. The hardest cases are no sweat to
God. "You don't know my husband ... my children ... my
boss." No, I don't, but the hardest cases are no problem to
God. Is it your heart's desire and constant prayer to God
that people be saved?

ABUNDANCE OF LOVE

And this I pray, that your love may abound still more and more in knowledge and all discernment, that you may approve the things that are excellent, that you may be sincere and without offense till the day of Christ, being filled with the fruits of righteousness which are by Jesus Christ, to the glory and praise of God (Phil. 1:9-11).

This really fascinates me! What a wonderful prayer. The heart of it is that we can expect an abundance of love. Do you believe that God's people need love? I think some of us need love so badly that we can't even express it to anyone. I'm not talking about romantic love. Many of us just need someone to care about us.

Does the world need love? Does it ever! With every passing year, I notice that society is more hostile. People need love. Perhaps someone in your life right now needs love more than you know. God answers prayer.

"This I pray, that your LOVE may abound still more and more .... " You never have too much love. You never have more than you need. Love melts the coldest heart. Love does wonders! You can meet a total stranger who is angry and hostile and love will melt that heart. The opposite is true, too.

We need to be people dominated by love. The Bible tells us that the greatest thing in life is love. Of all the wonderful attributes, love is the greatest. It is *"the more excellent way"* and though you could do great exploits for God, without love, they profit you nothing. You aren't accomplishing any good without love.

Knowledge **puffs** up, but it is love that **builds** people up! Love tells discouraged, weary people that they can go on another day. Love says, "No matter how you've failed, I forgive you and I want to help you to keep on going." Love encourages; it doesn't tear people down. We really need love.

"This I pray, that your love may abound more and more."

Chapter Four

HOW SHOULD WE PRAY?

Than He spoke a parable to them, that men always ought to pray and not lose heart, saying: "There was in a certain city a judge who did not fear God nor regard man. Now there was a widow in that city; and she came to him, saying, 'Avenge me of my adversary.' And he would not for a while; but afterward he said within himself, 'Though I do not fear God nor regard man, yet because this widow troubles me I will avenge her, lest by her continual coming she weary me.'"

Then the Lord said, "Hear what the unjust judge said. And shall God not avenge His own elect who cry out day and night to Him, though he bears long with them? I tell you that He will avenge them speedily. Nevertheless, when the Son of Man comes, will He really find faith on the earth?"

Also He spoke this parable to some who trusted in themselves that they were righteous, and despised others: "Two men went up to the temple to pray, one a Pharisee and the other a tax collector. The Pharisee stood and prayed thus with himself, 'God, I thank You that I am not like other men—

*unjust, adulterers, or even as this tax collector. I
fast twice a week; I give tithes of all that I possess.'
And the tax collector, standing afar off, would not so
much as raise his eyes to heaven, but beat his breast,
saying, 'God be merciful to me a sinner!' I tell you,
this man went down to his house justified rather than
the other; for everyone who exalts himself will be
abased, and he who humbles himself will be exalted"*
(Lk. 18:1-14).

In answer to the question, "How should we pray?" I give
you two words—habit and humility.

It is interesting that Jesus would use the unjust judge to
picture the just God of all the earth. He told us that this
woman who continually knocked at the door of the judge
represents those who continue to come to the Lord and ask
Him to answer prayer. Then, He followed it up with a
whole lesson on humility.

PRAYER IS A PROBLEM WHEN:

- We have sin that we do not confess and forsake.
- We have an unforgiving spirit.
- There's a wrong relationship between husband and
  wife.
- We lack faith.

Unconfessed Sin

Maybe the reason God is not answering prayer in your
life is one of those four things. Mind you, God has given

believers access into His presence regardless of whether or not we deal with our sin. We've been forgiven and cleansed and justified and sanctified, and we have access into His presence on the basis of the blood of our Lord Jesus Christ. We thank God for that. I can come directly to God because Jesus died and paid for my sin.

Nevertheless, sin that is entertained and coveted and kept in the heart, sin that we refuse to deal with, does become a hindrance to prayer. God may receive us and listen to us, but He has certain rules and standards by which He operates. When there is sin in our hearts that we will not confess and forsake, God has indicated in His Word that this is going to hinder our prayer life.

If I regard iniquity in my heart, The Lord will not hear (Ps. 66:18).

One who turns away his ear from hearing the law, Even his prayer shall be an abomination (Prov. 28:9).

He who covers his sins will not prosper, But whoever confesses and forsakes them will have mercy (Prov. 28:13).

There is only one message from God as to what we should do about sin. Everything was settled at the cross as far as our forgiveness is concerned. There is nothing to change at the cross. We're to acknowledge our sin before God and repent of it. That means: Stop! We're to **change our minds** about continuing in it, **change our conduct** about doing it, and **stop!** Prayer will always be a problem when sin is not confessed, when sin is not forsaken.

When we decide that we do not need to listen to the law of God, another one of the laws of God comes into play: Prayer becomes an abomination. God simply refuses to answer our prayers when we decide we don't want to listen to what His Word has to say about sin.

An Unforgiving Spirit

I don't know how many people are beset by an unforgiving spirit or how high on the list of sins this one is, but I have a feeling that it is a "biggy". There are people around us that will fail us. They will not live up to our expectations, or their own. People sometimes don't perform the way we want them to or the way we believe they should.

My friend, an unforgiving spirit is a terrible thing. An unforgiving spirit assumes that somehow the person does not **deserve** our forgiveness. I can clear that up! **Nobody** deserves to be forgiven! The other day I was talking to a gentleman who has suffered a repeated offense. As we were talking, I commented that he didn't seem to think that the offender deserved his forgiveness. He said, "You're right! They don't deserve to be forgiven because they keep doing it over and over again!" I shared with him that **he** didn't deserve forgiveness, either. He said he hadn't done anything wrong, so I pointed out that when he said that, he did something wrong. We **all** do wrong so his statement was a lie.

Aren't you glad that God forgives us—just wipes the slate clean? A lot of us haven't understood that so we hesitate to apply forgiveness to somebody when WE are offended. It's a very interesting problem.

*If you forgive men their trespasses, your heaven-
ly Father will also forgive you. But if you do not forgive men their trespasses, neither will your Father
forgive your trespasses* (Matt. 6:14).

How we relate to other people in terms of forgiveness is a
principle that affects our prayer life. If you're not con-
vinced about that read on.

*Then Peter came to Him and said, "Lord, how
often shall my brother sin against me, and I forgive
him? Up to seven times?" Jesus said to him, "I do
not say to you, up to seven times, but up to seventy
times seven.*

*"Therefore the kingdom of heaven is like a cer-
tain king who wanted to settle accounts with his servants. And when he had begun to settle accounts,
one was brought to him who owed him ten thousand
talents. But as he was not able to pay, his master
commanded that he be sold, with his wife and
children and all that he had, and that payment be
made. The servant therefore fell down before him,
saying 'Master, have patience with me, and I will
pay you all.' Then the master of that servant was
moved with compassion, released him, and forgave
him the debt. But that servant went out and found
one of his fellow servants who owed him a hundred
denarii; and he laid hands on him and took him by
the throat, saying, 'Pay me what you owe!' So his
fellow servant fell down at his feet and begged him,
saying, 'Have patience with me, and I will pay you
all.' And he would not, but went and threw him into*

*prison till he should pay the debt. So when his fel-
low servants saw what had been done, they were
very grieved, and came and told their master all that
had been done. Then his master, after he had called
him, said to him, 'You wicked servant! I forgave you
all that debt because you begged me. Should you
not also have had compassion on your fellow servant, just as I had pity on you?' And his master was
angry, and delivered him to the torturers until he
should pay all that was due to him. So My heavenly
Father also will do to you if each of you, from his
heart, does not forgive his brother his trespasses"*
(Matt. 18:21-35).

One writer said that Jesus told us to forgive others 490
times. No! That doesn't mean to count; it means that we
should forgive others endlessly! It doesn't matter how
many times they offend us, trespass against us, sin against
us, Jesus said, "Forgive them!"

Offhand, what would you say Jesus and the Heavenly
Father think of an unforgiving spirit? Is it a small problem?
No, I don't think so, either.

Is there somebody that you are totally unable to forgive?
Does someone come to mind? Forgive them RIGHT NOW
on the basis of what Jesus has forgiven you. Don't wait for
them to crawl to you and beg forgiveness. On the basis of
what Jesus has done for you—nothing else—forgive them
right now. Some people think we should wait until they
truly repent. Some people won't repent!

I remember two elderly ladies in a church I pastored who
had a grievance and both insisted that the other one was

wrong. They were both sure that they were right and it went on and on. To my knowledge, they both died without ever having settled it. I just want you to know that it is now settled in heaven where they both went to be with Jesus—they were both Christians. It is now settled.

Why are we eating our hearts out? The day we die the whole thing will be settled, anyway. I think some of us have such deep bitterness that we think we'll get these things **resolved** in heaven. Not at all! You won't even be discussing it because **it won't be an issue** anymore. The moment you die, the problem is settled—it's all settled. Why can't you do that now?

> *"Take heed to yourselves. If your brother sins against you, rebuke him; and if he repents, forgive him. And if he sins against you seven times in a day, and seven times in a day returns to you, saying, 'I repent,' you shall forgive him"* (Lk. 17:3-4).

The problem with this text is that it doesn't tell us what to do if he **doesn't** repent. I know a host of Christians who say that it means you don't forgive him unless he repents. It doesn't really say that, but we sort of conclude it from this text. On the basis of Matthew 18, we have to conclude the **opposite!** We have to conclude that if we have been forgiven by a master to whom we owe more, the least we can do is to forgive someone else whether he repents or not.

There is a problem with what we call "cheap forgiveness". Somebody comes and says they're sorry for some terrible thing and we just say, "OK. That's OK with me." Often we don't really mean it and continue to harbor resentment. Unforgiveness can eat you alive!

A gentleman who literally had money in six figures taken from him by another Christian said, "The only way I can forgive him is if he pays it back." I did some quick math. "He can't live long enough to pay you back!" I said. The man said that he should at least try to pay him back, and I agree. That would be a wise thing for the other man to do.

What if he never repents? What if he never pays it back? What if nobody ever says they are sorry? What if they keep doing it? Then what are you going to do? When we apply forgiveness, we want to think of what the OTHER person is doing—repenting, resolving things, getting right with the Lord. What if they never do it?

Aren't you glad the Lord doesn't treat us that way? He doesn't punish us according to our iniquities. He forgives us on the basis of what His Son has done, and He is the one in the story who forgave the larger debt. What He has done for us is the motivation for us to forgive other people.

I like what one writer says, "No one ever knows the depths of forgiveness until the person never repents."

A lot of people would like to set me straight on this point. I really do believe that you ought to try to get things straightened out, if you've offended somebody. You ought to try to resolve it, and the Christian attitude is to get it straightened out and to seek the forgiveness of anyone we've offended. I believe all of that, but I've seen good Christian people who have been offended and have been literally eaten alive by an unforgiving spirit. They wonder why they don't receive the blessing of God in prayer. An unforgiving spirit is a problem in the issue of prayer.

Wrong Relationship Between Husband and Wife

Likewise you husbands, dwell with them with un-derstanding, giving honor to the wife, as to the weaker vessel, and as being heirs together of the grace of life, that your prayers may not be hindered (I Peter 3:7).

In this particular case, the burden of proof is on the hus-band, not on the wife. *"Likewise"* refers back to statements telling wives to be submissive to their husbands and ser-vants to be submissive to their masters. *"Likewise"* hus-bands be submissive to the Lord!

Husbands are to be **submissive to their wives** by dwell-ing with them *"with understanding"*.   All husbands will agree that it takes understanding to have a submissive spirit toward their wives. Men are submissive to their wives by **trying to understand them**. Most women think their hus-bands won't give them the time of day!

The second way a man submits is by **giving honor to the wife.** He's already been told by God that he is the head of the home, so it's interesting that God tells the "head of the house" that he is not the one who will be honored. It is the one under him that is to be honored! *"Give honor to the wife."* Do you want to be lifted up? Do you want to be honored? Then be a servant of all!

Don't think she will get a "big head" if you honor her too much! Let God handle that! God has unique ways of deal-ing with that sort of thing. What God told a HUSBAND to do is to *"honor your wife"*.

It also says that you are *"heirs together of the grace of life"*. That means that **you are partners** in what God has done in your life. Husbands aren't better than their wives.

The next phrase is, *"... that your prayers may not be hindered."* The Greek word is *"to cut off"*. That's pretty strong! According to the Bible, the prayers of husbands are cut off when they do not understand or honor their wives—when they think they are better than their wives.

A Lack of Faith

Prayer is always a problem when there is a lack of faith. I guess most of us are aware of this and we are troubled about it. How much faith do you need? Jesus spoke about little faith, and great faith, and we wonder where we stand on the scale. A lack of faith produces ineffective prayer.

> *And when they had come to the multitude, a man came to Him, kneeling down to Him and saying, "Lord, have mercy on my son, for he is an epileptic and suffers severely; for he often falls into the fire and often into the water. So I brought him to Your disciples, but they could not cure him." Then Jesus answered and said, "O faithless and perverse generation, how long shall I be with you? How long shall I bear with you? Bring him here to Me." And Jesus rebuked the demon, and he came out of him; and the child was cured from that very hour. Then the disciples came to Jesus privately and said, "Why could we not cast him out?" So Jesus said to them, "Because of your unbelief; for assuredly, I say to you, if you have faith as a mustard seed, you will say*

to this mountain, 'Move from here to there,' and it
will move; and nothing will be impossible for you.
However, this kind does not go out except by prayer
and fasting" (Matt. 18:14-21).

Jesus almost sounds impatient! Note, too, that he **didn't**
say they failed because they hadn't been to seminary or
hadn't taken the latest course on the occult.

I was in the Holy Land at Bethany where Lazarus' tomb
is located. As you walk up the road, there are some mustard
plants. One of the men in our tour group, a young married
man, went over and took one of the seeds off and and he
called our attention to it. "That's really small! Jesus said if
you only have that tiny, little faith ... " I interrupted him to
point out that he was not looking at the mustard seed. I took
it from him and broke it open. Inside there were thousands
of little specks. "THAT is the mustard seed!" He commented that we don't believe much! You could hardly see
the tiny speck of mustard seed. Jesus said that if we have a
tiny speck of faith, we can move mountains!

We really have VERY LITTLE FAITH. The Bible says
that *"without faith it is impossible to please God." "He who*
comes to God must believe that He is and that He is the
rewarder of them that diligently seek Him." Why don't we
see God work in miraculous and powerful ways? Jesus said
it is because of our unbelief.

Now in the morning, as He returned to the city,
He was hungry. And seeing a fig tree by the road, He
came to it and found nothing on it but leaves, and
said to it, "Let no fruit grow on you ever again."
And immediately the fig tree withered away. Now

when the disciples saw it, they marveled, saying, "How did the fig tree wither away so soon?" So Jesus answered and said to them, "Assuredly, I say to you, if you have faith and do not doubt, you will not only do what was done to the fig tree, but also if you say to this mountain, 'Be removed and be cast into the sea,' it will be done. And all things, whatever you ask in prayer, believing, you will receive" (Matt. 21:18-22).

Here were the disciples with the Son of God and they had seen unbelievable miracles, and they were surprised that the fig tree dried up! "How did that happen?" they wondered. Talk about idiots! But you and I have done the same, and we know it. Jesus said, "If you have faith, AND DO NOT DOUBT, you will do this and move mountains, too! All things, whatever you ask in prayer, believing, you will receive." Do we, in fact, believe?

PRAYER IS A PRIVILEGE TO BE CULTIVATED IN THE PRIVATE LIFE OF THE BELIEVER

"But you, when you pray, go into your room, and when you have shut your door, pray to your Father who is in the secret place; and your Father who sees in secret will reward you openly. But when you pray, do not use vain repetitions as the heathen do. For they think that they will be heard for their many words. Therefore do not be like them.

*For your Father knows the things you have need
of before you ask Him. In this manner, therefore,
pray:*

Our Father in heaven,

Hallowed by Your name.

Your kingdom come.

Your will be done

On earth as it is in heaven.

Give us this day our daily bread.

And forgive us our debts,

As we forgive our debtors.

And do not lead us into temptation,

But deliver us from the evil one.

*For Yours is the kingdom and the power and the
glory forever. Amen.*

*For if you forgive men their trespasses, your
heavenly Father will also forgive you. But if you do
not forgive men their trespasses, neither will your
Father forgive your trespasses"* (Matt. 6:6-15).

I believe that the effectiveness of your prayer life is never
seen in public. I believe in public prayer and I believe that
Christians ought to get together to pray. However, the real
battle takes place in the private place where no one knows.
That's where the war is going on. That's where you find out
about prayer.

It's interesting that in verses 16-18, He says the exact
same thing about fasting! I ran into a fellow I know in

Chicago at a conference who looked terrible. He hadn't had any sleep. He hadn't shaved in a number of days. His hair was disheveled. His suit was all crumpled and his tie was wrinkled. He had come to a pastor's conference and I happened to see him. I asked if he had a problem. He said, "I've been fasting! I've been before God. The only way to find spiritual power is to fast." I was kind of hungry because it was just before lunch. I didn't know what to do but I couldn't help mentioning that Matthew 6 says he should have cleaned himself up before going out in public. He didn't remember what it said, so I read it to him:

> *"Don't be like the hypocrites, with a sad countenance. For they disfigure their faces that they may appear to men to be fasting. Assuredly, I say to you, they have their reward. But you, when you fast, anoint your head and wash your face, so that you do not appear to men to be fasting, but to your Father who is in the secret place; and your Father who sees in secret will reward you openly"* (Matt. 6:16-18).

"I think you've blown your reward," I told him. Maybe that man was sincere, but there is only one fast commanded in the Bible. It was pharisaical words that spoke of fasting twice a week. We had better be careful not to get into the legalistic ritual of fasting in order to somehow know more of the power of God. I think real fasting is when you get so involved in ministering that you forget to eat! Sometimes, when you're studying or praying, you can go long hours without food and you don't make a big deal about it. You also make sure nobody else knows about it, either. That's what it is to fast!

When we ask how to pray, we are aware that many Christians have never learned how to pray privately. We actually need a public group in order to pray. There's our weakness. We all need to learn that our Father *"who sees in secret"* will reward us openly. He wants to know what you're like when no one is looking. Your character is what you are in the dark. Your reputation is merely what people think you are.

PRAYER WAS A PRIORITY WHEN THE CHURCH BEGAN

Then they returned to Jerusalem from the mount called Olivet, which is near Jerusalem, a Sabbath day's journey. And when they had entered, they went up into the upper room where they were staying: Peter, James, John, and Andrew; Philip and Thomas; Bartholomew and Matthew; James the son of Alphaeus and Simon the Zealot; and Judas the son of James. These all continued with one accord in prayer and supplication, with the women and Mary the mother of Jesus, and with His brothers. And in those days Peter stood up in the midst of the disciples (altogether the number of names was about a hundred and twenty) (Acts 1:12-15).

They were there for ten days and the primary thing they were doing, was praying.

*And they **continued** steadfastly in the apostles' doctrine and fellowship, in the breaking of bread, and in prayers* (Acts 2:42).

Prayer was a priority when the church began. **They prayed for wisdom in selecting leaders.**

> *And they proposed two: Joseph called Barsabas, who was surnamed Justus, and Matthias. And they prayed and said, "You, O Lord, who know the hearts of all, show which of these two You have chosen to take part in this ministry and apostleship from which Judas by transgression fell, that he might go to his own place." And they cast their lots, and the lot fell on Matthias. And he was numbered with the eleven apostles* (Act. 1:23-26).

It wasn't Paul that became the twelfth apostle—it was Matthias. The Holy Spirit even agrees with that in Acts 2:14 where it says Peter stood up *"with the eleven"* long before Paul met Jesus on the Road to Damascus. Whenever we need to select leaders, we should pray.

> *"Therefore, brethren, seek out from among you seven men of good reputation, full of the Holy Spirit and wisdom, whom we may appoint over this business; but we will give ourselves continually to prayer and to the ministry of the word." And the saying pleased the whole multitude. And they chose Stephen, a man full of faith and the Holy Spirit, and Philip, Prochorus, Nicanor, Timon, Parmenas, and Nicolas, a proselyte from Antioch, whom they set before the apostles; and when they had prayed, they laid hands on them. And the word of God spread, and the number of the disciples multiplied greatly in Jerusalem, and a great many of the priests were obedient to the faith* (Acts 6:3-7).

Now in the church that was at Antioch there were certain prophets and teachers: Barnabas, Simeon who was called Niger, Lucius of Cyrene, Manaen who had been brought up with Herod the tetrarch, and Saul. As they ministered to the Lord and fasted, the Holy Spirit said, "Now separate to Me Barnabas and Saul for the work to which I have called them." Then, having fasted and prayed, they laid hands on them, they sent them away. So, being sent out by the Holy Spirit ... (Acts 13:1-4).

The first missionary team was born in prayer.

So when they had appointed elders in every church, and prayed with fasting, they commended them to the Lord in whom they had believed (Acts 14:23).

Elders were chosen. Missionaries were selected. Elders at the church in Jerusalem were elected. Someone to replace Judas was called out. Whenever there was a need for leaders, they prayed—they prayed for wisdom in selecting leaders.

They also prayed for boldness in the midst of persecution.

And being let go, they went to their own companions and reported all that the chief priests and elders had said to them. So when they heard that, they raised their voice to God with one accord and said: "Lord, You are God, who made heaven and earth and the sea, and all that is in them, who by the mouth of Your servant David have said:

*'Why did the nations rage, And the people plot
vain things? The kings of the earth took their stand,
And the rulers were gathered together Against the
Lord and against His Christ.'*

*"For truly against Your holy Servant Jesus,
whom You anointed, both Herod and Pontius Pilate,
with the Gentiles and the people of Israel, were
gathered together to do whatever Your hand and
Your purpose determined before to be done. Now,
Lord, look on their threats, and grant to Your servants that with all boldness they may speak Your
word, by stretching out Your hand to heal, and that
signs and wonders may be done through the name of
Your holy Servant Jesus." And when they had
prayed, the place where they were assembled
together was shaken; and they were all filled with
the Holy Spirit, and they spoke the word of God with
boldness* (Acts 4:23-31).

In Long Island, New York, at a meeting where I spoke, a
young man sang who is called, "The Subway Singer". His
name is James Humphrey. He is from a whole family of
lawyers, but he got saved and decided that something else
needed to be done besides legal work. He plays a good
guitar and he also plays a harmonica, so he hooked a harmonica around his neck and plays them both at once. He
also sings and writes all of his own music. He is well
known all over New York because he works the subways
where all the violence is—Grand Central Station, Times
Square. He sings up a storm and tells people about Jesus.
He's been doing it for years. What a delight he was!

Talk about persecution! He's had a lot of it. I asked him what he does when he's persecuted. "I pray," was his answer. He's just a little guy. Sometimes they take his guitar and smash it. Then, he buys another one, he said. His only way of handling all that violence is to pray. That's all! He looked like a lamb going into a den of lions to me. I liked him a lot. God has protected that young man in an unusual way. The police don't want him there because his life is in danger. That's OK with him because those people need the Lord.

He had a cute little song about the "Subway Circus" in which he describes all the "wierdos" and "wackos" in the New York subways. You hear about all of them and at the end it says, "But God loves them and they need the Lord." The wierdest, most awful, most violent people in the world are there, but this young man believes that somebody has to tell them that God loves them. God has not given us *"a spirit of fear, but of power, and of love and of a sound mind."* As he sees it, the most important thing he needs is prayer. That comes out of the early church!

They also prayed for protection and deliverance. If you're scared about something, do what the early church did—pray! Prayer was a priority for the early church.

> *Peter was therefore kept in prison, but constant prayer was offered to God for him by the church. So, when he had considered this, he came to the house of Mary, the mother of John whose surname was Mark, where many were gathered together praying. And as Peter knocked at the door of the gate, a girl named Rhoda came to answer. When*

she recognized Peter's voice, because of her glad-
ness she did not open the gate, but ran in and an-
nounced that Peter stood before the gate. But they
said to her, "You are beside yourself!" Yet she kept
insisting that it was so. So they said, "It is his
angel." Now Peter continued knocking; and when
they opened the door and saw him, they were
astonished (Acts 12:5,12-16).

They said, "That can't be Peter! That's what we're praying for!" Have you ever been astonished that God answered
your prayers? It's happened to me.

I was preaching in a small, country church back East and
the church of about a hundred people had been praying for
revival. They wanted folks to be saved. It was way back in
the hills where they pipe in sunshine and pipe out moon-
shine—one of those kind of places. I had a wonderful time
with those people. God blessed the meetings in a marvelous
way in that little mining town. Folks got saved and one
night, over a hundred people were saved. Now, all they had
in the church was a hundred people so that doubled the number in one night! One man said, "We prayed, but this is getting ridiculous!" He was concerned that they didn't have
enough coffee for everyone after the service.

The early church prayed and God answered, and they
were astonished!

They prayed for enouragement and support, too.
Paul was meeting with the church leaders at Mileta and this
story is one of the sweetest passages of Scripture. Their
relationship, the peer group prayer and the friends told of
here is beyond anything the world knows.

And when he had said these things, he knelt down and prayed with them all. Then they all wept freely, and fell on Paul's neck and kissed him, sorrowing most of all for the words which he spoke, that they would see his face no more. And they accompanied him to the ship (Acts. 20:36-38).

That passage makes me cry. Those people had a relationship that has been lost in the church today. *"They knelt down and prayed."* The love that was there was notable. God encouraged Paul's heart.

*When we had sighted Cyprus, we passed it on the left, sailed to Syria, and landed at Tyre; for there the ship was to unload her cargo. And finding disciples, we stayed there seven days. They told Paul through the Spirit not to go up to Jerusalem. When we had come to the end of those days, we departed and went on our way; and they all accompanied us, with wives and children, till we were out of the city. And we knelt down on the shore and praye*d (Acts 21:3-5).

We can't help noticing that the early church prayed—it was encouraging and supportive in difficult times. *"They knelt down on the shore and prayed."*

They also prayed for food. This is an interesting story of shipwreck.

And when he had said these things, he took bread and gave thanks to God in the presence of them all; and when he had broken it he began to eat. Then they were all encouraged, and also took food themselves (Acts 27:35-36).

Somebody asked me if there is anything in the Bible that says that they thanked God for their food. Oh yes! Prayer is connected with the generosity of God in providing our food. In talking about what will happen in the last days, food is part of what Paul discussed.

*... forbidding to marry, and commanding to abstain from foods which God created to be received **with thanksgiving** by those who believe and know the truth. For every creature of God is good, and nothing is to be refused if it is received with thanksgiving; for it is sanctified* [set apart for our use] *by the word of God and prayer* (I Tim. 4:3-5).

The early church prayed for **wisdom** in selecting leaders, **boldness** in the midst of persecution, **protection and deliverance, encouragement and support,** and they prayed **for food.**

PRAYER IS A PRACTICE IN WHICH CHURCHES SHOULD CONTINUALLY ENGAGE

Now I beg you, brethren, through the Lord Jesus Christ, and through the love of the Spirit, that you strive together with me in your prayers to God for me, that I may be delivered from those in Judea who do not believe, and that my service for Jerusalem may be acceptable to the saints, that I may come to you with joy by the will of God, and may be refreshed together with you (Rom. 15:30-32).

This is group prayer—*"strive together with me in your prayers to God."* Should Christians get together in groups and pray? Yes!

> *Praying always with all prayer and supplication in the Spirit, being watchful to this end with all perseverance and supplication for all the saints* (Eph. 6:18).

Churches as groups are to pray!

> *For I know that this will turn out for my salvation through your* [plural, not singular] *prayer and the supply of the Spirit of Jesus Christ* (Phil. 1:19).

> *Be anxious for nothing, but in everything by prayer and supplication, with thanksgiving, let your* [plural again] *requests be made known to God; and the peace of God, which surpasses all understanding, will guard your hearts and minds through Christ Jesus* (Phil. 4:6-7).

There are plenty of Christians who do not believe that the church should give itself to corporate, public prayer. That's why I'm emphasizing this point. They say that you can't prove that in the Bible, but I say the exact opposite is true!

> *Continue earnestly in prayer, being vigilant in it with thanksgiving; meanwhile praying also for us, that God would open to us a door for the word, to speak the mystery of Christ, for which I am also in chains* (Col. 4:2-3).

All of this is using the plural forms—Paul is asking a whole church at Colosse to pray for his team. You find this all through the epistles.

Prayer is to be both private and public, and it is good to get on our knees, both privately and publicly. It is a reminder to us of what really is important. I have preached all over America about prayer. I want you to know that there are very few churches doing anything more than having the pastor pray in their services. We all know that, but the Bible teaches that we should ALL pray.

I don't know if you pray in private or not. That is where you should learn to pray. You need to pray to the Lord in private, but we also need to pray as a group. One of the greatest needs of the church today is to get together and pray. Whatever work we have to do will go much better if we get on our knees and talk to God about it. We need to pray. There should never be a meeting (any kind of meeting) of Christians, without prayer.

Chapter Five

MEN OF PRAYER

Therefore I exhort first of all that supplications, prayers, intercessions, and giving of thanks be made for all men, for kings and all who are in authority, that we may lead a quiet and peaceable life in all godliness and reverence. For this is good and acceptable in the sight of God our Savior, who desires all men to be saved and to come to the knowledge of the truth. For there is one God and one Mediator between God and men, the Man Christ Jesus, who gave Himself a ransom for all, to be testified in due tiime, for which I was appointed a preacher and an apostle—I am speaking the truth in Christ and not lying—a teacher of the Gentiles in faith and truth.

Therefore I desire that the men pray everywhere, lifting up holy hands, without wrath and doubting; in like manner also, that the women adorn themselves in modest apparel, with propriety and moderation, not with braided hair or gold or pearls or costly clothing, but, which is proper for women professing godliness, with good works. Let a woman learn in silence with all submission. And I do not permit a woman to teach or to have authority over a man, but to be in silence. For Adam was formed first, then

*Eve. And Adam was not deceived, but the woman
being deceived, fell into transgression. Nevertheless
she will be saved in childbearing if they continue in
faith, love, and holiness, with self-control* (I Tim.
2:1-15).

This is one of those passages which most preachers, including myself, break down into little pieces. There is a
good reason for it—there are a lot of issues in it about
women's dress, and submission, and whether women can
teach or not, and about Adam and Eve, and childbearing.
What happens is that we focus on the particular issues and
miss the overall context. I want to talk about the overall
context which is the most important thing about this chapter.

Paul wrote to Timothy who was in charge of several
churches. He wrote about how the churches should be or-
ganized and how they should run. One of the major issues
he dealt with is in chapter two. You'll see that it is or-
ganized in two parts. Therefore, there are two points that I
want to make concerning it. The first seven verses are one
paragraph. The second paragraph begins with *"therefore"*
and this is correct although the New International Version of
the Bible leaves out this word. Paul is saying, "In the light
of what I said in the first seven verses, I am now going to
make an application."

The second half of the chapter is putting into action,
describing, what kind of spiritual leadership was spoken of
in the first seven verses. These first verses tell us of the
need for spiritual leadership in the life of men. The last verses describe for us the nature of that leadership. I want you
to see the overall context which is that one of the

most important things a church can even think about doing, is praying.

When Paul gave Timothy instructions on how to manage a church, he said that he had to get the men to pray if he was to have a church which honored Jesus Christ.

THE NEED FOR SPIRITUAL LEADERSHIP

The first thing Paul wrote about was prayer. He made it clear that **prayer had to be a priority** in the lives of the men of the church. *"Therefore I exhort first of all ... "* doesn't mean that this is the first thing Paul was going to talk about because he had already talked about some things. This means that the top priority was to be prayer—above all else. When Paul talked about what was important, prayer went to the top of the list. *"... first of all ..."* means *"above anything else"*. The first and most important priority in a man's life is prayer. That's what the Bible says.

We also need to note that **this priority centers in prayer and praise.** He said in verse one, *"... supplications* [urgent needs], *prayers* [worship—praying toward God], *intercessions* [intimate requests], *and giving of thanks.* If a man really understands spiritual leadership and it is a priority in his life above everything else, it centers in prayer and praise.

The word *"intercessions"* is used only one other time and that is in I Timothy 4:3-5. There we see what is meant by *"intercessions"*. Literally, *"intercessions"* means *"to fall into something"* and it carries the idea of one-on-one communication.

Prayer involves **supplication** which means expressing an urgent need. It is the cry of a man who knows he cannot handle things and needs to call upon God.

Prayer involves **worship** which means giving thanks toward God.

Prayer also involves **intercession.** I Timothy 4 talks about what will happen in the endtimes. It says that there will be those who advocate a kind of asceticism which is not of God.

> ... *forbidding to marry, and commanding to abstain from foods which God created to be received with thanksgiving by those who believe and know the truth. For every creature of God is good, and nothing is to be refused if it is received with thanksgiving; for it is sanctified* [made special] *by the word of God and prayer* (I Tim. 4:3-5).

Why is the food I eat made special when I give thanks? The word of God makes it special because you are expressing thanks to God who made it possible for you to have the food. That deals with your heart. The food is also set apart (made special) by the very act of prayer. The last word of verse 5, *"prayer"*, is the same word *"intercession"* (I Tim. 2:1) and those are the only two places in the Bible it is used.

That means a "one-on-one intimacy" where you sense that you are grateful to God even for a sandwich that you eat. One of the serious problems of male leadership in our society is our refusal to pray (whether public or private) for our meals. I exhort every man who has any sensitivity to God and His Word to make a commitment in his heart that—whether public or private, whether by yourself or with a group of people, whether it is official or not—you will always give a prayer of thanksgiving for your food. I've seen such a prayer in a public place become a door to open a conversation about spiritual things. Many Christian people don't pray at their meals.

I was with a group of pastors in Arizona and we were sitting around a table—five other pastors and myself. It was a crowded restaurant and it was noisy. One of the pastors said, "Why don't we just pray silently? We don't want to give any offense." He shouldn't have done that. My friend next to me put his hand on mine and said, "David! Don't do what I think you're going to do!" It ticked me off to think of praying silently! I stood up and called everyone to attention. Then, I asked everyone to be quiet since it was such a noisy restaurant. I couldn't believe it! Everyone around us got quiet and bowed their little heads! I had an audience, so I prayed through the whole gospel, finished praying and opened my eyes to find my fellow pastors hiding under the table.

Men of God need to thank God for our food. It is a simple matter.

After *"intercessions"*, it says, *"... giving of thanks ...."* This centers in praise and thanksgiving to God. What I see in our "macho" world is a lot of complaining. In answer to, "Hi! How are you? How did your day go?" we go on at length about how hard the hassles have been. We like to make things sound really rough. I find guys complaining about everything when we need to be men of thanksgiving! We are to give thanks and praise God for whatever is happening in our lives.

A lot of things are in category "Bad", but we need to smell the roses and look at the trees, and thank God for His wonderful blessings. What a wonderful thing it would be in the American family to have a father who wasn't complaining all the time! We need fathers who are not negative, but positive—who are giving thanks for all things. "Thank you, Lord! You have been so good to us!" Children need to be raised in a home where the man prays and gives thanks to God constantly. We need that kind of gratitude.

A man's spiritual leadership also has **a special purpose.** *"... that we may lead a quiet and peaceable life in all godliness and reverence. For this is good and acceptable* [well pleasing] *in the sight of God our Savior, who desires all men to be saved."* Not only is the **stability of society** involved in a man praying, but it will also have an effect on society in allowing the freedom of the gospel s**o that people may be saved.** That's the natural implication of these verses.

THE NATURE OF THIS SPIRITUAL LEADERSHIP

Verse eight begins with *"therefore"*. It is in the Greek text and has the meaning of *"I desire"*. It doesn't mean, "I wish ...", "I hope you will ...", or "I consider it to be a creative alternative ...." The Greek word means *"reason"* and *"counsel"*. Paul was saying, "I am **instructing** you on the basis of **sound reason,** in the light of the need for prayer, that men should pray."

There is a major problem in this passage that is affecting all of society today. Recently I read of a change in the

Methodist hymnal. They now are getting rid of songs like "God of Our Fathers" and anything that mentions the male image of God. I want you to know that God is a Father! He also acts like a mother! The church of Jesus Christ throughout history has made one colossal mistake on this issue. It comes out of this passage and I Corinthians, chapters 11 and 14.

In this passage it says that women are to be submissive to men. That's what it says, and we have to discuss it. It says that they are to learn in silence. I Corinthians 14 says that if they want to learn anything, they are to ask their husbands at home. She may think he doesn't know anything, but she is to ask him anyway!

One fairly new Christian man who is really "macho" came up to me and said, "I have a question. No, it really is my wife's question, but I'm not letting her talk to you!" I was amused and asked him why. His answer was the verse from I Corinthians which says she is to ask him at home. "But I don't know nothin'!" was his next remark! "If you tell me, and I tell her, then she'll think I DO know somethin'." I thank God for a man like that—that's what we're supposed to do!

The problem in church history, unfortunately, is that they taught that **all** women are to be submissive to **all** men. That applies in many of today's churches in that women can't sit on any board—no leadership position. They cannot teach adults—only children. Some churches think they might go a little further and say that women can teach adult women, but not men.

Today, people are asking if women can be ordained and become pastors. Interesting question! Lots of women are saying they are tired of male domination and they want to share in the leadership of the church. In the Methodist denomination, one half of all the preachers are women. There is a shortage of men taking leadership in the Methodist church.

We have a problem in our society, and I do not agree with church history. I do not believe that the Bible teaches that **all women** are to be submissive to **all men**. We have been WRONG on that and we need to admit that we have been wrong.

I'm saying this because the Bible says only ONE thing: A woman is to be submissive to HER OWN husband— nobody else's husband! When you stretch it to mean "all women" and "all men", you get yourself in trouble. I believe that there are only two things that restrict women in the ministry of the church: They cannot be an elder or a bishop because it says that an elder must be "a husband" and "a father". Why would God do that? If I were a woman, I would thank God He set it up that way. Guess who God's going to "zap" if things go wrong! He's going to "zap" the men! The women are protected because they don't bear the responsibility before God. God has that in the church because He wants the church to be seen as a family and the father is the one who is responsible in the family.

Could a woman be a pastor? Not usually, because the pastor is also considered to be an elder. However, I want you to think about the possibility of having an all male board of elders ("husbands and fathers") who recognize a woman's teaching and preaching ministry, not making her an elder, but giving her their approval to teach and preach. This is possible. There are women in the Bible who were teachers and preachers. There are women prophets in the Bible. In the New Testament, we see women teaching and preaching in Corinth (I Corinthians 11). Can a woman teach and preach with adults there (men and women)? Of course!

The second requirement is that she is submissive to her husband. If a woman is submissive to her husband and does not hold the position of a bishop or an elder, there is no restriction on them in the local church. We've got to be honest about that! We have to deal with that.

I know two women who teach, but only one is submissive to her husband. It doesn't matter how long that woman talks, she is a blessing. The other, who is not submissive to her husband, finds that after thirty seconds the men in her audience are uncomfortable. The issue has always been the same! The Bible says a woman is to be submissive to her **own** husband—not all women submissive to all men. We made that up! It was part of a chauvinistic, male-dominated society and I think the sooner we get rid of it, the better.

On the other hand, I don't want anyone outside of the church telling us whether or not a woman can be on the Board of Elders. The Bible has already settled that. We can't take submission out of the wedding vows, either. That isn't what the Bible says. We want to stick with what the Bible says.

This is a very controversial passage because it delineates the roles of men and women without identifying whether or not this is man and wife. I'm on thin ice here and there are a lot of good men who disagree with me. Please be open-minded enough to hear me out.

The Bible was written in Greek, not English. In Greek, there is only one word for a woman or a wife, married or un-married. You can't tell by the Greek word whether a wife is meant or not. There has to be something else in the context to tell you whether it means a wife or a woman in general. When it comes to a man, this is not so. There is a word for man in general and we get anthropology from that word. It can also mean "mankind" including both men and women. Is that the word in this text? If it were, it would be saying that all women are to be submissive to all men, but it is not!

Every time husband is meant in the Greek, you must use a particular word. **That** is the word that is in ALL THREE of the controversial passages in the New Testament. I do not believe the English translators were correct in saying *"women"* (in general) and *"men"* (in general) when, in fact, the issue is husband and wife.

> *"Therefore I desire that the [husbands] pray everywhere, lifting up holy hands, without wrath and doubting; in like manner also that the [wives] adorn themselves ... which is proper for [wives] professing godliness .... Let a [wife] learn in silence with all submission. And I do not permit a [wife] to teach or to have authority over a [husband] but to be in silence"* (I Tim. 2:8-12).

It makes all the difference in the world as to how you interpret the passage! What is the issue? It speaks here of men of prayer. Is there a need for spiritual leadership? Yes! We read of it in verses 1-7. What is the nature of that leadership? The answer is in verses 8-15. I'm going to give you six words that will analyze the nature of a man's leadership that Paul gives us here.

CONSISTENCY

In verse 8, we read, " ... *that the [husbands] pray EVERYWHERE.*" The Greek says, *"in every place"* and that can mean location or situation (circumstance). Let's look at it again. *"I want [husbands] to pray in every [location or situation, whatever it is]."* In other words, God is emphasizing the importance of men being leaders in prayer with their families all the time—in every situation and in every place. The husband is to take the leadership in prayer.

Why should the wives be praying with the children when they go to bed and when they get up in the morning? Why aren't the husbands doing that? Why should the wife take the leadership of praying at the table? Why doesn't the husband do that? The Bible teaches that the husband and the father should do that.

Saying that you believe in praying but not actually praying is NOT consistency in your life! The Bible teaches that we should be consistent in praying.

CONSECRATION

It says in verse 8, " ... *lifting up holy hands ...."* I don't like to skirt around issues. I'm not trying to be controversial, but there are a lot of traditions that teach us to lift our hands in worship. I'd like to comment on that for a moment.

We often focus on the physical, outward act and miss the point. It says, "... *lift up HOLY hands* ...." By the way, it didn't tell the wives to do this; it tells the husbands to do this. As I observe things, there are a lot of women doing this even though it really says for the men to do it.

I believe that there is a real important act of worship that both the Old and New Testament constantly focus on. It tells us to *"bow the knee"* and we do very little of this. I don't believe that I have, in reality, *"bowed the knee"* just because I get on my knees before God. It doesn't mean that I am broken and humble before God just because I got on my knees. Why do I do it then? Sometimes it isn't appropriate and I don't want to kneel just to be a show; however, in private, I believe that is a great practice. Nobody is there to impress, but the physical act of kneeling reminds us of who we are in relationship to God. **A physical act expresses the attitude of our hearts.**

Lifting up our hands can also be **a physical expression** of our hearts before God. If we only do it to be seen, we're making a big mistake. In Psalm 22, we have an example of David praying and crying to the Lord, **lifting up his hands** to God. In Psalm 63:3-4, we have the example of praise.

Because Your lovingkindness is better than life,
My lips shall praise You. Thus I will bless You while
*I live; I will **lift up my hands** in Your name.*

Is the point to lift up my hands? I think something else is involved. If you stop focussing on *"hands"* and emphasize *"lift up"*, suddenly your mind is open. Throughout the Psalms it speaks of *"lifting up the soul to God"*. How do we express that physically?

> *Bow down Your ear, O Lord, hear me; For I am*
> *poor and needy. Preserve my life, for I am holy; You*
> *are my God; Save Your servant who trusts in You!*
> *Be merciful to me, O Lord, For I cry to You all day*
> *long. Rejoice the soul of Your servant, For to You,*
> *O Lord, I lift up my soul* (Ps. 86:1-4).

There are many examples of the relationship between each of us and God, and when we talk about men in spiritual leadership praying, there must be consecration there. *"Lifting up holy hands"* means that a man is walking with the Lord. *" ... HOLY hands..."* means men whose prayer life is effective because they walk with God and stay away from sin. There is consecration there whether the man ever lifts up his hands or not! It is only **a physical reminder** that our whole heart needs to be in tune with God.

CONTROL OF TEMPER

Verse 8 says that husbands are to *"lift up holy hands, without wrath ...."*

> *And you, fathers, do not provoke your children*
> *to wrath, but bring them up in the training and ad-*
> *monition of the Lord* (Eph. 6:4).

Nothing discourages and defeats the heart of a child like a father's anger. If he blows his stack, loses control, pounds his fists, or hits his kids anywhere except on the bottom, he has provoked them in a way God never intended. That kind of hostility in husbands and fathers is a major sociological problem in our country right now. There is so much hostility in our homes that it is a wonder that any kid stays around! The rebellion we see among our children is what they have learned at home—swearing, shouting, blowing up at the slightest thing. This kind of behavior doesn't make sense even to the child!

Spiritual leadership on the part of men who know how to pray to God is without anger. Such men are able to control their tempers. If you can't control yours, you have **a serious spiritual problem** which demands that you get on your knees with a broken heart and get right with God! Confess your sin to your family and your children, and seek their forgiveness for the anger that you've had.

CONFIDENCE IN THE LORD

Verse 8 continues by saying that the husbands are to pray with holy hands, without anger and without doubting.

If any of you lacks wisdom, let him ask of God, who gives to all liberally and without reproach, and it will be given to him. But let him ask in faith, WITH NO DOUBTING, for he who doubts is like a wave of the sea driven and tossed by the wind. For let not that man suppose that he will receive anything from the Lord; he is a double-minded man, unstable in all his ways (James 1:5-8).

You may say you're praying and talking to God and that God can answer prayer. However, if you don't believe it in your heart, it is doubting. The Bible says that those of us who come to God must believe that He is and that He is the rewarder of those who diligently seek Him. When you pray, do you have confidence in the Lord?

What is spiritual leadership? It is **consistency, consecration, control of temper,** and it is **confidence** in the Lord.

CONCERN FOR HIS WIFE'S NEEDS

Have you wondered why verses 9-12 are in I Timothy 2? It's almost like a parenthesis. Verse 8 tells the men to pray, then verse 9 says, *"... in like manner ...."* Clearly, it is telling the wives to do the same thing as the husbands, in the same way. They are to *"adorn themselves in modest apparel"* and *"to learn in silence with all submission".* What are the major needs of wives as given in this chapter? Two things are given and this is **a message to the husbands,** not to the wives.

A basic need of every wife is **to display her beauty in a godly manner.** I am sick and tired of pastors (like me) who use these passages to beat women over the head! That shows me that they have not studied the passage! It is instructing **men** about prayer and spiritual leadership and, according to God, it says that the man is responsible for how the woman looks! Why is this connected to a man's prayer life? Why does it follow the command to *"lift up holy hands"*? He is responsible!

The Bible teaches that women are to be beautiful. It certainly doesn't tell them to be ugly! I'm not discussing jewelry or hair style. I'm here to tell every man that spiritual leadership **includes** being concerned with his wife's need which is to display her beauty in a godly manner that does not embarrass you or any other man. You walk with God and your wife is a showcase of your commitment to the Lord. You don't turn her into some ugly thing that looks like she needs help. You are definitely concerned that she be beautiful, and you never want anyone to sense seduction or sensuality in her.

The second need of a wife is also very serious. She needs to be able **to depend on her husband.** Most wives can't! Wives get beat up for not submitting when there is nothing to submit to! There are two dangers in the hearts of wives in regard to their need to depend on their husbands. First, there is **a natural tendency for her to take over.** That's what this passage is dealing with and it usually happens because of her husband's reluctance, or failure, to take the leadership. She doesn't know what else to do. She cares about her children and her family, so she doesn't just let it go to pieces. She steps in and does it. It's a natural tendency, but God is warning you about this. That's why He says *"to learn in silence with all submission"*.

Does that mean that you don't talk? No! The Greek has a word for that and it is **not** found here. It's not talking about a cessation of words; it's talking about **a tranquility of heart** that is submissive to your husband. Sure you can talk to your husband and communicate with him! Still, you're depending upon his leadership. You know that the final decision rests with him and that he is accountable before God. God will take care of him. You can say, "Honey, I think you should do such-and-such, but whatever you think the Lord wants you to do is fine with me." Please don't add that God will "zap" him if he makes the wrong decision!

The second danger is that **a woman will be deceived.** Women should not be upset or bitter about this tendency— God made women that way. Women have a sensitivity about things that a man doesn't have and he needs to learn this from his wife. She has a tendency to be deceived like Eve was, but don't throw roses to Adam—he deliberately disobeyed God! He knew what was right and he still disobeyed.

The point here is very important for a man's spiritual leadership. He needs to know that if he isn't filling his role, his wife's tendency will be to take over and she may not understand many issues especially as they relate to men. She can be deceived.

The basic needs of a wife are to display her beauty in a godly manner and to **depend** upon her husband. Most men don't care about the beauty of the women in their families and that has gotten us into the mess we're in. Men have failed to take the spiritual leadership in the family and wives need to depend on their husbands. What do we hear on television, movies and from our friends? The exact opposite! "Be independent! He'll let you down."

By the way, **his basic need** is to depend on his wife, but we aren't talking about that in this passage—we're talking about husbands.

Men who know how to pray, also care about their wives' needs. Men who walk with God know the issues involved. Men need to pray.

COMMITMENT TO CHRIST

A man can't be a spiritual leader if he isn't personally **committed to Christ.** We find that in verse 15. Here is a controversial passage which talks about Adam and Eve.

Because of Eve's deception, she fell into transgression. Well then, was she saved?

Nevertheless she will be saved in childbearing if they continue in faith, love, and holiness, with self-control (I Tim. 2:15).

At this point, I must tell you that, if you have some of the new versions, you have an incorrect English translation and those translators know it. It's unfortunate because they tried to interpret this passage. They tried to make it say that women will be kept **physically** through the experience of childbearing although there is no plural word for "women" in this passage. It is singular! *"She"* refers to Eve. The Greek says she will be saved through THE childbearing.

That's referring to the promise God gave to her that a seed would come from her (the woman) and bring salvation to all in this world. This is a reference to the Messiah—the Incarnation when God became Man, when Jesus was born. He was the Deliverer and that is how Eve was to be saved along with all the other women in the history of the world.

"... if they continue in faith, love, and holiness, with self-control" is not saying that your salvation depends on your acceptable deeds. That's a "class condition" and means that, if you really are saved, others will see *"faith, love, and holiness, with self-control"* in your life.

I look at this text and I praise the Lord! Do you know what every man needs to be a spiritual leader? He needs the same thing his wife needs—a personal commitment to Jesus Christ! The only salvation possible to any of us is through Jesus Christ our Lord—the Way, the Truth and the Life. No one comes to the Father except through Him.

Chapter Six

A Woman of Prayer

Now there was a certain man of Ramathaim Zophim, of the mountains of Ephraim, and his name was Elkanah the son of Jeroham, the son of Elihu, the son of Tohu, the son of Zuph, an Ephraimite. And he had two wives: the name of one was Hannah, and the name of the other Peninnah. Peninnah had children, but Hannah had no children. This man went up from his city yearly to worship and sacrifice to the Lord of hosts in Shiloh. Also the two sons of Eli, Hophni and Phinehas, the priests of the Lord, were there. And whenever the time came for Elkanah to make an offering, he would give portions to Peninnah his wife and to all her sons and daughters. But to Hannah he would give a double portion, for he loved Hannah, although the Lord had closed her womb.

And her rival also provoked her severely, to make her miserable, because the Lord had closed her womb. So it was, year by year, when she went up to the house of the Lord, that she provoked her; therefore she wept and did not eat. Then Elkanah her husband said to her, "Hannah, why do you weep? Why do you not eat? And why is your heart grieved? Am I not better to you than ten sons?" So Hannah arose after they had finished eating and drinking in Shiloh.

Now Eli the priest was sitting on the seat by the doorpost of the tabernacle of the Lord. And she was in bitterness of soul, and prayed to the Lord and wept in anguish. Then she made a vow and said, "O Lord of hosts, if You will indeed look on the affliction of your maidservant and remember me, and not forget your maidservant, but will give your maidservant a male child, then I will give him to the Lord all the days of his life, and no razor shall come upon his head."

And it happened, as she continued praying before the Lord, that Eli watched her mouth. Now Hannah spoke in her heart; only her lips moved, but her voice was not heard. Therefore Eli thought she was drunk. So Eli said to her, "How long will you be drunk? Put your wine away from you!" And Hannah answered and said, "No, my lord, I am a woman of sorrowful spirit. I have drunk neither wine nor intoxicating drink, but have poured out my soul before the Lord. Do not consider your maidservant a wicked woman, for out of the abundance of my complaint and grief I have spoken until now." Then Eli answered and said, "Go in peace, and the God of Israel grant your petition which you have asked of Him." And she said, "Let your maidservant find favor in your sight." So the woman went her way and ate, and her face was no longer sad.

Then they rose early in the morning and worshiped before the Lord, and returned and came to their house at Ramah. And Elkanah knew Hannah his wife, and the Lord remembered her. So it came to pass in the process of time that Hannah conceived and bore a son, and called his name Samuel, saying, "Because I have asked for him from the Lord." And the man Elkanah and all his house went up to offer to the Lord the yearly sacrifice and his vow. But Hannah did not go up, for she said to her husband, "I will not go up until the child is weaned; then I will take him, that he may appear before the Lord and remain there forever." And Elkanah her husband said to her, "Do what seems best to you; wait until you have weaned him. Only let the Lord establish His word." So the woman stayed and nursed her son until she had weaned him.

Now when she had weaned him, she took him up with her, with three bulls, one ephah of flour, and a skin of wine, and brought him to the house of the Lord in Shiloh. And the child was young. Then they slaughtered a bull, and brought the child to Eli. And she said, "O my lord! As your soul lives, my lord, I am the woman who stood by you here, praying to the Lord. For this child I prayed, and the Lord has granted me my petition which I asked of Him. Therefore I also have lent him to the Lord; as long as he lives he shall be lent to the Lord." So they worshiped the Lord there (I Sam. 1:1-28).

There's a Jewish proverb that says, "God couldn't be everywhere, so He made mothers." That isn't theologically correct, but you get the idea that mothers are important! Even when we look at that beautiful harbor that brings so many immigrants to our shores and see the magnificent Statue of Liberty done by the sculptor, Bartholdi, a lot of us forget that his model was own mother. Many advised him to do otherwise, but he chose to do it that way. That is our Statue of Liberty.

Suzanna Wesley had seventeen children and she had a ritual every morning during which she was not to be interrupted—no matter what happened. The children had to defend her in this. They had to explain to anybody that came to the door that their mother was not available until the hour was up. It was exactly an hour that she took every morning to pray for her children. She refused to be interrupted during that time. It was a law in her home. She went into a private place and did not allow any of the children to come in and for that hour, she prayed for all seventeen of her children. No wonder that two of them turned the world upside down and affected our constitutional republic more than our schools are willing to teach. Two of her sons were John and Charles Wesley.

My mother practiced what I preach! My earliest memory of my mother as a young boy was seeing her on her knees, praying for me. At the baby shower given her before I was born, others tell me that she asked the pastor to pray that God would not only bring me to Jesus Christ but make me a preacher and teacher of the Word of God. She never told me that until I grew up and decided to become that on my own. God does wonderful things through prayer and a lot of us need to understand that **prayer is what moves the heart of God.**

We need to understand about the power and priority of prayer. We must not think that we are wasting our time when we pray. The Bible tells us about prayer and assures us that God is near to all those who call upon Him. The heart of God is delighted when people pray. He tells us to call on Him *"while He may be found"*. He told us to *"call unto [Him] and [He] will answer"*. We need the Lord and prayer is the way to draw near to Him.

THE PROBLEM SHE FACED

This story has a lot of insights for our families. It shows us how they faced a problem within the family. Hannah had to try to find a way to endure her situation.

It Was A Marital Problem

> *And he had two wives: the name of one was Hannah, and the name of the other Peninnah* (I Sam. 1:2).

One is enough! The Bible does not authorize anyone to have more than one wife. The fact that it was a cultural thing does not justify multiple wives. God made it clear to Solomon that he should never have more than one wife. Solomon violated his commitment to the Lord and it cost him dearly, for those women took his heart away from God. This man, Elkanah, was wrong in this even though they had a devout and religious home. There are many devout and religious homes today, but that does not mean that they don't have problems.

This man went up from his city yearly to worship and sacrifice to the Lord of hosts in Shiloh (I Sam. 1:3).

Shiloh (Joshua 18:1) is the site where the Tabernacle of the Lord was placed when Joshua brought the Children of Israel into the land of Canaan after the death of Moses. Those people conquered the thirty-one kings in the Land of Canaan. The Bible says they set up the Tabernacle at Shiloh long before they ever made Jerusalem their capitol and built Solomon's temple there. The Tabernacle of the Lord was at Shiloh and that's where everybody came to worship.

Elkanah's home was a devout and religious home, but they had a marital problem—he had two wives.

It Was A Physical Problem

Hannah had no children (verse 5), and it also tells us that *"the Lord had closed her womb"*. A lot of people are not ready to understand or accept the sovereignty of our God even in the matter of family size and having children. A lot of us have questioned God's ways in this regard. My friend, God is in charge and He knows why the events of our lives happen the way they do.

"All things come from Him and are through Him and shall be unto Him."

"He works all things after the counsel of His own will."

Greater things are accomplished by God controlling all things (even though we don't always agree) than if man were in total control. We trust our sovereign God who (the Bible says) *"does whatever He pleases in heaven and on earth"*.

The beautiful part of this story is that the Lord answers prayer, but make no mistake about it, *"the Lord had closed her womb"*. Why didn't she have any children? God saw to it and didn't allow any children to be born to her. He knew what His purpose was and, today, we all rejoice in seeing it because we learn about prayer and how God answers.

What a blessing that child was! Samuel was the last of the judges of Israel. They were in a period of transition in which everyone *"did that which was right in his own eyes"* (Judges 21:25). There was utter chaos, anarchy and rebellion. It was a terrible time changing from the rule of judges in Israel to the period of the kings of Israel. Samuel was the transition person for all of that and he was the one who anointed Israel's first king, Saul. Samuel was the last of the judges and the first of the prophets who gave moral and spiritual direction to the kings of Israel.

When we look at Hannah we wonder why she had to suffer so much. She was deeply disturbed over this. It was a marital problem for her and a physical problem.

It Was An Emotional Problem

And her rival also provoked her severely, to make her miserable, because the Lord had closed her womb (I Sam. 1:6).

The interesting thing to me is that all of this emotional conflict and turmoil happened at the place of worship. It was stirred at those times of worship when joy and praise should have filled their hearts. Instead, there were deep emotional problems in Hannah's life and in her family. There was envy, suspicion, jealousy, and provoking and bitterness in this devout, religious family. Listen! Just because you go to church doesn't mean that you are right with God! Just because you listen to the Word of God being preached doesn't make everything right at home. There are problems in our lives and we hear the Word of God so that we will know what God has to say about them. Then, we try to put what we learn into practice in our daily lives.

Elkanah and his family were faithful in attending the worship services of the Lord. They also had problems and there was constant tension between the two wives. Not having children was a shame and disgrace in Israel because the whole system of inheritance was built on having children. The woman, Hannah, lived with that shame.

Elkanah wasn't helping! He gave Hannah a *"double portion"*. After they made their offerings to the Lord, they ate the food that had been offered. It was a wonderful time of celebration. The families sat around the table in order to celebrate and worship and praise the Lord. Imagine watching as Elkanah gave Hannah two times as much as anyone else just because she had no children! It stirred feelings of bitterness and resentment as to why she was being treated so well when she had no children to contribute to the family. Imagine what Peninnah said! "I gave you sons and daughters and look at the way you treat her!" Elkanah loved

Hannah, but *"the Lord had closed her womb"* and there wasn't anything he could do about it.

In verse 7, it says that she *"wept and did not eat"*. We're talking about a severe emotional problem and Hannah could hardly deal with it. She couldn't eat and she was crying her heart out. Elkanah, the husband, was not very helpful! *"Why do you weep? Why do you not eat?"* Men always want to know **why** their wives are crying. Impatiently, they say, "Just tell me! I'll understand!" Oh, sure!

What a thing for Elkanah to say, *"Am I not better to you than ten sons?"*! The woman was wise enough not to answer him because the answer is, "No!" As a matter of fact, she didn't like the marital situation; she didn't like the problem of having no children; she didn't like the constant conflict in their home. No, Elkanah was NOT better than ten sons! Being a spiritual woman, she didn't say that.

THE PRAYER THAT SHE MADE

In the case of her problem, she was finding it difficult to endure daily life. It was not easy. She sought the Lord's help with her problem. Do you go to the Lord when you've got a problem? "Take all your burdens to the Lord and leave them there." *"Cast your burden on the Lord, and He will sustain you."* Do you spend all your days in anxiety about the problems in your life, or do you take it to the Lord in prayer? Hannah's prayer was her way of seeking the Lord in her life.

It Was A Serious Concern

And she was in bitterness of soul, and prayed to
the Lord and wept in anguish (I Sam. 1:10).

This problem was eating Hannah up! This was a severe,
uncontrollable situation. This was the kind of woman who
could not keep from crying—and it wasn't from joy. These
words are very strong in the Hebrew text. Hannah was
losing control. Her heart was filled with bitterness and
when she called out to God, it was a deep and serious burden on her heart. She couldn't handle it any more. Life is
like that.

There are foonotes along the way through this text about
the religious situation in Israel.

This man went up from his city yearly to worship
and sacrifice to the Lord of hosts in Shiloh. Also the
two sons of Eli, Hophni and Phinehas, the priests of
the Lord, were there (I Sam. 1:3).

Now Eli the priest was sitting by the doorpost of
the tabernacle of the Lord (I Sam. 1:9).

The religious situation in Israel was not good in those
days. Here was a woman who loved the Lord and a family
that came regularly to worship, but the priesthood was not
good. Eli could not control his sons and this book goes on
to tell us that these young men were "making it" with every
woman that came in the door. Talk about television scandals
in our day? They had it in Israel long ago. These men were
immoral.

They were treating the sacrifices of the Lord improperly and they took their own "cut" out of the pie. They lacked integrity and honor before God. They lacked holiness. This was a pitiful situation! God severely rebuked Eli for not disciplining his boys when he raised them. That family was out of control, and they were running the worship services! God took away the priesthood from that family and *"Ichabod" ("the glory has departed")* is what was pronounced on Eli's family because of the wickedness of Hophni and Phinehas, his two sons. The priesthood was taken out of their hands and put into the hands of another family because of the disobedience, rebellion and rottenness of that home.

That's the kind of setting in which Hannah poured out her heart to God.

It Was A Specific Commitment

When you make a vow to God, do not delay to pay it; For He has no pleasure in fools. Pay what you have vowed. It is better not to vow than to vow and not pay (Eccles. 5:4-5).

Then she made a vow and said, "O Lord of hosts, if You will indeed look on the affliction of your maidservant and remember me, and not forget your maidservant, but will give your maidservant a male child, then I will give him to the Lord all the days of his life, and no razor shall come upon his head" (I Sam. 1:11).

It's a little risky to make this kind of vow to God. The Hebrew is a play on words, *"She vowed a vow"*.

Samuel must have grown up to look like some of our contemporary musicians! The issue here, however, is not whether or not his hair was long, it was part of a commitment in God's law called the Nazarite Vow. It was dealing with the issue of separation. To emphasize that separation, there were distinct restrictions, one of which was never to cut that person's hair at all. Everybody who saw Samuel knew that he was under the Nazarite Vow. That implies that other people cut their hair and they all knew the difference. The Nazarite was never to cut his hair. He was totally given to the Lord.

No, Samuel didn't have any say-so in it. Do think some attorney should have come forward to defend his rights? This was a vow that a mother made to God for a child she didn't even have yet. It was quite a commitment.

My mother made the same vow to the Lord. Nobody asked me about it. I thought early in my life that I would go into music. I liked that a lot. One day, I opened the Bible and started to realize how wonderful it is! I memorized Scripture and I studied the Bible and it never really dawned on me what God had in mind, but my mother knew all the time. She had made a vow in her heart to the Lord. I imagine there were many days when she wanted to tell me that I was going the wrong way! She never once said to me that I was supposed to be a preacher and teacher of the Bible. I always wanted to share God's Word—that was in my heart! I wanted to do it, but I didn't know what my mother had in her heart. I'm not saying that the only reason I'm a preacher

was my mother's prayers, but it certainly had a lot to do
with it.

Hannah made a commitment to the Lord. She took a
chance. *"I'll give him to You all the days of his life."*

> *Eli thought she was drunk. So Eli said to her,*
> *"How long will you be drunk? Put your wine away*
> *from you!"* (I Sam. 1:13-14).

I feel that the priest, in his accusation, was an absolute
outrage! Talk about spiritual discernment! He hadn't
bothered to find out why the woman was upset. He just
jumped to the conclusion that she was drunk because she
was so upset. The man was far from God and he deserved
the punishment that God gave him.

THE PEACE SHE RECEIVED

She had peace, after she prayed, even though the answer
had not yet come. Can you get peace in your heart when
your problem has not yet been resolved? Oh yes! It's like
the eye of a hurricane. There is perfect calm even though all
hell is breaking out around you. Hannah had peace because
she trusted the Lord's plan for her.

In the case of her **problem**, she had to endure a difficult
situation. In the case of her **prayer**, she sought the help and
the will of the Lord. She couldn't go on like that anymore.
The **peace** that she received was to trust the Lord's plan for
her. Interestingly, the assurance came from the old priest,
Eli, himself.

Her Assurance From Eli

> *Then Eli answered and said, "Go in peace, and*
> *the God of Israel grant your petition which you have*
> *asked of Him"* (I Sam. 1:17).

That was an acknowledgement from the leader (poor as he was with his own family) who recognized the **will** of the Lord and the **hand** of the Lord. Those priests would wait upon God, by the way, in their service in the Tabernacle, right in front of the Altar of Incense from which smoke ascended symbolizing their prayer to God. They brought the requests of the people before the Lord and God would often manifest His answers and His presence by what is called the *"Shekinah glory of God"*. It was like a cloud that came down over the Tabernacle. Many people would wait outside to see it as the priests went about their duties, pleading the cases of the people to the Lord. They waited for God to answer.

We also know that God spoke directly to the priests. We don't know all of what went on here "between the lines" so to speak. We do know that when Jesus was born, his cousin (John the Baptist) was born into a priest's home. We know that Zachariah, John's father, was waiting to hear the voice of the Lord in his regular priestly duty when God spoke after four hundred years of slience.

The Jews were very excited about that because God was silent from the end of the Old Testament until the time of John the Baptist. Priests continued to do what they always did every day, but God did not speak. The glory had departed, and part of that story is right here in this story of Hannah. The glory had left Israel at the time of the Babylonian captivity and there were four hundred silent years.

Here, Eli was performing his service in the Tabernacle and he brought the request of that dear woman to God. He burned the incense on the Altar as he was required to do, and offered her prayer to God. There was some kind of a manifestation from God that told him that God was going to give her a child. He walked out and told Hannah to go in peace, that God was going to give her the request that she had made.

The **assurance** came from the priest, Eli, but notice her **attitude**.

Her Attitude of Humility

And she said, "Let your maidservant find favor in your sight." So the woman went her way and ate, and her face was no longer sad (I Sam. 1:18).

She humbled herself and called herself a *"maidservant"* and even wanted favor in the eyes of that poor priest. She went back to her difficult situation filled with the peace of God even though there still was no child! She had **peace** that God would answer her prayer. Beautiful!

THE PRAISE SHE OFFERED

She endured her **problem.** She sought God in **prayer.** She received **peace.** She **praised** the Lord for who He is and what He can do.

Then they rose early in the morning and wor-
shiped before the Lord, and returned and came to
their house at Ramah. And Elkanah knew Hannah
his wife, and the Lord remembered her. So it came
to pass in the process of time that Hannah conceived
and bore a son, and called his name Samuel, saying,
"Because I have asked for him from the Lord" (I
Sam. 1:19-20).

"They" rose early—her husband was in on this! Two
things strike me, and I'm sure they struck you as you read
that, too.

The Lord Remembered Her Need

Aren't you glad that God never forgets? God knows
what your need is. He knows what you need, even before
you ask Him! Do you wonder if God knows about your
pain? The Bible tells us that He knows and what's more, He
cares! It says so over and over again! He knows the sparrow
that falls from the tree and all the hairs of your head are
numbered. He knows it all! This statement reminds us of
that.

Has the Lord ever remembered you and answered your
prayer? A sweet thing happened to me. My mother was
taken into the hospital for a serious condition, and she'd already been in a convalescent home for a couple of years.
She'd had surgery on a growing infection problem and they
felt they couldn't do surgery again. It was getting worse and
I hated to see her in that condition. We prayed that God
would take care of the problem because it was very serious.

One morning, as I was there very early, the doctor showed up at the same time. We both wanted to see if the antibiotics they were giving her had worked. As we were standing there beside her bed, all of the infection poured out of her body! I watched a miracle of how God can answer prayer when God's people call upon Him.

I read her the story of Hannah and she said, "God answers prayer, David, and you're one of them!" I saw that God could answer prayer in the midst of a painful, agonizing situation even though we knew that the only permanent solution is the resurrection of the body. It was tender of the Lord to move in our lives when He doesn't have to. **The great deliverance** is His return, but He moved in and did something special for us just to let us know that He remembers us. Hallelujah to our God!

Hannah thanked the Lord! She worshiped the Lord! The Lord not only **remembered her need, He answered her prayer.**

The Lord Answered Her Prayer

There's a little note about the name, Samuel, that I want to bring to your attention. Some people say that Samuel means "to ask from the Lord", but it doesn't. *"El"* on the end is, of course, the word, "God". The first part, however, means *"to hear"*—not to ask. There's a very important point there. It was because God HEARD that the answer came! It wasn't because she ASKED! What an important difference to understand!

Did she ask? Yes! But the reason she was given a child was not BECAUSE SHE ASKED, it was BECAUSE GOD HEARD!   That's the difference between man-centered theology and God-centered theology.   Are you following what I'm saying? Too much emphasis is often put on the person, so if you don't get what you ask for, others say that you don't have enough faith. My friend, **it's not great faith in God that gets answers to prayer. It's faith in a great God!** It's God who hears and answers. He said so!

My experience has been that God blesses in spite of me and not because of me. We need to understand that. Hannah did! God heard her prayer, and He answered the cry of her heart. Everytime anyone saw Samuel, Hannah wanted people to remember that God answers prayer!

THE PLAN SHE HAD

And the man Elkanah and all his house went up to offer to the Lord the yearly sacrifice and his vow. But Hannah did not go up, for she said to her husband, "I will not go up until the child is weaned; then I will take him, that he may appear before the Lord and remain there forever" (I Sam. 1:21-22).

Her plan was to nurse and train the child. At what age do mothers usually wean a child? We don't usually talk about these things, but in those days, the earliest was about three years old and the latest was about five or six. In certain cultures today, children are nursed up to eight and ten years old. I've seen it myself in some of the countries in Africa, especially. For Samuel, it was probably about three to five years old. We're talking a very small boy when Hannah gave him up. During those early years, she nursed him.

It reminds me of the story of Moses. When the daughter of Pharoah found the baby in the bulrushes, Miriam got his own mother to nurse him. The Bible speaks in a wonderful way about the influence of his mother upon Moses just in those early years of his life.

Psychologists tell us that most of what a child is going to understand and his patterns of life are primarily developed before he is five years old. Whether that is true or not, I don't know. I do know that many, many of us understood before we were five years old that we were sinners and needed to be saved. We heard the gospel of Jesus Christ— that He died for our sins on the cross and that He rose again from the dead. In simple childlike faith, many receive Jesus as Lord and Savior in those early years.

Jesus took a child of pre-school age and set him in the midst of people and said, *"Of such is the kingdom of heaven."* He took little children into His arms, and blessed them. He said to His disciples, *"Forbid them not!"* God honors that. What Hannah did in the life of Samuel was special, too, and it affected his life forever. She nursed him and trained him—that was her plan.

Her husband's response is interesting. He could have said, "What do mean, 'Give up the child' after we worked so hard at having him? God blessed us and now you're going to let him go? He won't make any money being a preacher! Are you going to let him do that? Stop it! You're just emotionally upset, Hannah." Aren't you glad you don't read that in this story?

Lots of parents have failed to understand this story. Have you ever given your children to the Lord? They belong to Him, you know. The Bible calls children, *"the heritage of the Lord,"* and *"God's gift to you"*. They come from the Lord, you know that don't you? Don't ever separate the relationship of your children from God. God gave them to you for a little while, to train and love them, but you have to let them go when the time comes. You'll do it with fear and trepidation and when you let them go, you'll think they still need you—even though they act like they don't.

Sometimes you wonder if you did a good job of raising them. About the time you think you're an expert in this area, they are gone! You struggle most of your life to be the kind of parent you believe God wants you to be and you make a lot of mistakes. One day, you think you've gotten the hang of it, and they're gone! Hannah knew early what it was to be committed to the Lord. She gave all that she had, including her children, to God.

THE PROMISE SHE KEPT

Now when she had weaned him, she took him up with her, with three bulls, one ephah of flour, and a skin of wine, and brought him to the house of the Lord in Shiloh. And the child was young (I Sam. 1:24).

She had promised to give him to the Lord's work; that was her vow. If you have a New International Bible or the New American Standard, you will read that she went up *"with a three year old bull"*. Believe it or not, this little point has a lot to do with the story. Was there one animal, or three? The King James reads, *"three bulls"* which is based (1) on the Dead Sea Scrolls that read that way, (2) on the Septuagint (a translation of the Hebrew and the Greek) which also reads *"three bulls"*, and (3) the Masoretic Texts. They put vowel markings on the Hebrew language about 900 A.D. and the present Hebrew Bible is called the Masoretic Text. That also reads *"three bulls"*. So, I think it is incorrect to say *"a three year old bull"* and that the King James is accurate in saying, *"three bulls"*.

It also says, *"one ephah of flour and a skin of wine"*. They didn't need to bring that much. This is an interesting insight into this story. Hannah decided to do three times more than was required to indicate, I believe, her love and appreciation to God who answered her prayer. She went beyond what was required of her.

> *And when you prepare a young bull as a burnt offering, or as a sacrifice to fulfill a vow, or as a peace offering to the Lord, then shall be offered with the young bull a grain offering of three-tenths of an ephah of fine flour mixed with half a hin of oil; and you shall bring as the drink offering half a hin of wine as an offering made by fire, a sweet aroma to the Lord* (Num. 15:8-10).

Hannah brought **three times** as much as was required for the offering. What was she doing here? Why were they required to make a sacrifice when they made a vow? There's a little saying that I use to understand the sacrificial system of the Old Testament: "Every commitment you make to

God is preceded by the offering of a blood sacrifice which stands for cleansing." Little Samuel needed cleansing and she brought a sacrifice in obedience to the Lord.

Even if parents had made no vow, every child in Israel was to have a blood sacrifice offered. Every time anybody in Israel sinned against the Lord, they brought a blood sacrifice. There were sacrifices going on constantly in addition to the seven major feasts of Jehovah. They offered them all the time—every day. That's what priests were all about. They were constantly killing animals and having blood sacrifices. "Every commitment you make to God is preceded by cleansing."

You may want to serve the Lord and be all that God wants you to be, but you need to be cleansed in order to be used by God.

The grain offering was a meal which indicated your fellowship with God and your agreement with Him. They ate it with the family with praise and thanksgiving for what God had done. Yet, Hannah was giving up her boy on that occasion! Imagine that.

As many people have commented before me, there was only one reason for Hannah to do all of this—she was overwhelmed with gratitude and thanksgiving to God. She wanted to do at least three times what was required just to let everyone know that God answers prayer; God can do anything. Her heart overflowed with praise.

> *Honor the Lord with your possessions, And with the firstfruits of all your increase; So your barns will be filled with plenty, And your vats will overflow with new wine* (Prov. 3:9-10).

Hannah came to honor the Lord and she overdid it! What a celebration they had!

> *Then they slaughtered a bull, and brought the child to Eli. and she said, "O my lord! As your soul lives, my lord, I am the woman who stood by you here, praying to the Lord. For this child I prayed, and the Lord has granted me my petition which I asked of Him. Therefore I also have lent him to the Lord; as long as he lives he shall be lent to the Lord." So they worshiped the Lord there* (I Sam. 1:25-28).

Other translations say, *"I have given him to the Lord,"* or *"I have dedicated him to the Lord"*. These are good meanings. Saying, *"I have lent him to the Lord"* doesn't mean that she was going to take him back. She kept her promise. She gave him to the Lord.

One of the greatest things we can do is to give our children to God. Sometimes we put a footnote saying, "... for whatever they want to do". No, it should be "... for whatever **God wants to do** in their lives".

"Train up a child in the way he should go" (Prov. 22:6) doesn't mean the way **his parents** want him to go. Just because you're a fireman, don't expect him to be a fireman. Just because you're a businessman, he doesn't need to be a businessman. That command doesn't mean that he's to go the way **he** wants to go, either. We worry about directing our children in ways that don't use **their talents**, but that isn't what it means, either!

When the term, *"the way"*, is used in Proverbs, it means, *"the way of the Lord"*. We're talking about morality, righteousness, justice, integrity, honor—*"The way of the Lord."* When he is old, he won't depart from it. It will remain in his heart forever because you trained him in the way of the Lord.

Some of us have never made **our own** commitment to God. Hannah did, and the **joy** that came to her heart and the **blessing** that came to her life as Samuel became the greatest of the prophets was tremendous. Samuel became the one who anointed God's king and he was the one so used of the Lord that God never let any of his words "drop to the ground". **All of this was because one woman prayed.**

We need to have a deep appreciation of how God answers prayer. If we are faithful in prayer, God will answer. His timing may be very different from ours, but He sees our grieving, troubled hearts. We can rest in the fact that **He is a God who answers prayer.** We can bring our grief and *"bitterness of soul"* to Him.

He will also accept our commitment to Him when we come to Him wanting His hand on our lives more than anything else. Let's make the commitments we know we should make through the wonderful open door God has given us called, "Prayer".